WHO KILLED COCK ROBIN?

Who Killed Cock Robin?

*British Folk Songs
of Crime and Punishment*

Compiled and edited by
Stephen Sedley and Martin Carthy

Published by Reaktion Books
and the English Folk Dance and Song Society

Published by
Reaktion Books Ltd
Unit 32, Waterside
44–48 Wharf Road
London N1 7UX, UK

www.reaktionbooks.co.uk

First published 2021
Arrangements and commentary © Stephen Sedley and Martin Carthy 2021

Published in association with the English Folk Dance and Song Society

Printed and bound in Great Britain
by TJ Books Ltd, Padstow, Cornwall

A catalogue record for this book is available from the British Library

ISBN 978 1 78914 503 8

CONTENTS

To the nameless and numberless
singers and musicians
who over the centuries
have created and tended
our tradition of song

PREFACES

STEPHEN SEDLEY

If traditional song reflects the things that most affect the lives of ordinary people, it's not surprising that love and the law loom large in it. Back in the 1960s, I compiled and edited *The Seeds of Love*, an anthology of traditional songs about love. Half a century later, the time seemed ripe for a parallel volume reflecting some of the ways in which life for many people has involved either dodging the law or careering headlong into it.

It was in those early years, when I was supposed to be studying law and starting out in practice as a barrister, that my interest in folk song brought me into contact with a number of traditional and revival musicians. One of the latter was the talented singer, scholar and instrumentalist Martin Carthy. We have been friends ever since, while Martin built a huge following, was a guest on *Desert Island Discs* and collected an MBE and an honorary doctorate of music, and I became first a jobbing lawyer and writer, then a judge, and still later a law professor. In addition to the contribution of material from his repertoire, Martin's guidance and advice have been indispensable in compiling this anthology.

My early research in the 1960s revealed troves of unpublished folk songs, many of them in manuscript collections, others printed on old (and often obscurely catalogued) broadsides, but many more still alive and well in the memories and voices of traditional singers. In the intervening years research has been transformed by the modernization of the Vaughan Williams Memorial Library at Cecil Sharp House, the digitization of manuscript collections and the creation of the online Roud Folk Song Index. To assist research, each song in this book a carries a footnote setting out the printed or oral sources we have used, its Roud Index number and, where relevant, its number in Francis J. Child's *The English and Scottish Popular Ballads* (which will also be its number in Bertrand Bronson's *The Singing Tradition of Child's Popular Ballads*). The select bibliography at the back lists the principal printed sources cited in short form in the notes to the songs.

In addition to library research, as a young barrister I would go to rural Kent to defend Travellers, evicted and barred from their traditional camping grounds on the commons, against repeated charges under the legislation then in force of 'being a gypsy encamped on a highway'. Getting charges thrown out because the police initially couldn't work out how to prove the accused was a Gypsy gave me a local status and an introduction to some fine singers. One of these, Joe Saunders, an old poacher and bird-breeder who lived mostly on Biggin Hill, turned out to have a large repertoire of prison, poaching and transportation songs, some of which, with the help of the Uher reel-to-reel tape recorder I carried in my car boot, appear in this book.

The allocation of individual songs to particular crimes or punishments is of course an editorial artifice, but it has made it possible to include some legal background in the introduction to each section, and some history and legal commentary in the notes to individual songs. Above all, Martin and I have tried to ensure that every song, whatever its sources, not only reads well but sings well. All, we hope, display the vivacity of Britain's centuries-old oral tradition of song. It is as well to keep in mind that, apart from the occasional song which has a known source, there is no single authentic version of any folk song.

Traditional song rarely adopts strict metre, preferring sometimes to follow the contours of the text and sometimes to respect the logic of the melody. Harmonic accompaniments, for their part, are best devised by performers.

It will be evident that the oral traditions from which this anthology is drawn are those of Scotland and England. Welsh traditional song has relatively few points of contact with these, while Irish song, which has a great many, needs a book to itself. In this situation orthography presents constant problems to which there is no uniform solution. We have followed the practice of reproducing dialect words or ellipses, but (with the exception of Tommy Armstrong's own dialect spellings in 'Durham Gaol') have not sought to mimic regional accent or intonation. Even this boundary, however, is porous: where 'hoonds' would legitimately be regarded as a crude anglicization of 'hounds', 'guid' is an accepted (because phonetically precise) Scots spelling of 'good'. An editor's only hope is to give as little offence as possible.

The editors have had valuable guidance from Peggy Seeger and Professor Ruth Perry on the provenance of some of the songs, from the late Professor Roger Hood CBE QC, and from professors Jeanette Neeson and Douglas Hay, on the history of English penal law. We have also had the skilled assistance of Corin Bagshaw in formatting the tunes, and of Dick Wolff both in transcription and in musicological research and advice. Any mistakes or misjudgements which remain are ours.

Readers should keep in mind that the legal commentaries are not only far from comprehensive but are based on the law of England and Wales. Scotland's criminal law has always been distinct.

Martin Carthy

The great English traditional singer and family friend Walter Pardon called the very large repertoire of songs that he carried 'Our History'. Often it amounted to an alternative history distinct from anything he had learned at school. When Walter first appeared in public he had not sung (so he said) in front of people for twenty-five to thirty years, and when he spoke to us about it, he said, 'I sang in Norwich Folk club and all those people listened and clapped, and then I sang at Norwich Folk Festival and there were hundreds of people and they all listened and clapped, and I cried and I cried.' He had kept the songs alive in his mind, and forgotten nothing, by rehearsing them to himself over and over again.

If experience has taught me anything, it's that people have no call to be embarrassed by their own music. There is no such thing as bad music – just bad musicians. But I've many times now had the good fortune to experience the reverse: the many fine singers and instrumentalists who, seemingly out of thin air, create and recreate songs and melodies of infinite subtlety.

I listen to a singer like Walter Pardon very carefully because his phrasing is gorgeous and I very often want to reflect that in the guitar playing. I like to play to the singing rather than the other way round and that requires changing one's attitude. Walter's small time-shifts, tiny pauses and so on present one with a subtlety that I think is worth emulating. He is a very beautiful singer, as are Sam Larner, Joseph Taylor, George Maynard and the brothers Jasper and Levi Smith, among dozens of others. We truly do stand on the shoulders of giants musically speaking.

Since Stephen has said some kind things about me in his preface, let me reciprocate. I recall the appearance in 1967 of his songbook *The Seeds of Love*, containing a wealth of previously unpublished material. As a young legal aid lawyer and part-time song collector he was coming for the first time into contact with material that, for each of us, added breadth and depth to the music we had come to love.

The longer I am involved in folk song, the more I am aware that tradition is in itself a work in progress, never an edifice. It has constantly to renew itself, with people ready and willing to run with the ideas it generates. People have always done so and continue to do so. This is their right, for it belongs to them.

POACHING

The protection of private property has for centuries been both a central purpose of the law and a source of popular anger and defiance. Trespass on private land was always a civil wrong; but neither Parliament nor the judges were able to make it a crime, because foxhunting unavoidably involved mass trespass by horses, hounds and hunters over whatever land the fox fled across. Nor were landowners generally able to claim ownership of the game on their land, since birds and beasts did not recognize estate boundaries. So it was by devising the crime of trespassing in search of game (foxes were classed as vermin) that landowners were able to distinguish between their friends and their foes and to have the latter trapped, gaoled, transported and sometimes even executed.

The rural population, restricted to taking what they could from commons eroded by centuries of enclosure (the fencing of previously open-access manorial heath and woodland), regarded the appropriation of game by landowners both as a violation of their natural rights and as a challenge to their courage and ingenuity. The nineteenth-century Leicestershire poacher James Hawker, in his memoirs, veers engagingly between the need to feed his family and the pleasure of out-witting the gamekeepers. But what to country folk was a group of lads going out on a moonlit night to take some game for the pot had by the eighteenth century become, to landowners and their MPs, an epidemic of armed gangs ready to violate property rights and fight gamekeepers to the death (as in 'The Oakham Poachers').

The so-called Black Act of 1723 (which remained in force until 1827) responded by making it a capital felony to walk out at night armed and disguised, typically by blackening faces – hence its nickname. In addition to creating some fifty other capital felonies, it allowed trials to take place in any county in order to minimize the risk of sympathetic local juries. Over thirty more game laws were added in the course of the eighteenth century, but poaching continued unabated, some-times becoming a local industry. Porters on the stagecoaches were bribed to carry poached game to London alongside the squire's gifts of game to family and friends. If the poached game became high, the porters would switch the labels.

Fanny Burney in 1789 recorded the gentry's fear that the game laws and church tithes could cause revolution to spread across the Channel. *The Shooting Directory* for 1804 actually described the underlying purpose of the game laws as 'the pre-vention of popular insurrection and resistance to the Government by disarming the bulk of the people'.

Landowners were not always innocent victims. It was not uncommon for them to let game birds and deer feed on their tenants' crops until dawn, when gamekeepers would drive them back into the squire's close, having first set angled spears at the boundary to impale any dogs which tried to follow (as in 'Thornymoor Woods'). Tenant farmers or smallholders, by contrast, were not entitled to take game straying on to their own land, for since the 1670 Game Act only the lords of manors, heirs to titles or estates, or owners of land producing £100 or more a year in income had been allowed to take game at all. Selling game for the table was forbidden.

Within the manorial estate, saw-toothed mantraps might be set. Another practice, not banned until 1861, was to set spring guns – firearms fixed in position and discharged by tripwires. Poachers responded by tracing the tripwires and re-setting the guns against the keepers. Taking deer (which were classed separately from game and were the landowner's property while on his estate) was a crime of a higher order, as the older ballads record, routinely carrying the death penalty.

The rural population sometimes showed a smart grasp of the laws that prioritized prosecutions and required fines to be paid over to informers. In the Cannock Chase area, for example, a poacher who knew he had been spotted would get a collaborator to lay an information – a charge – against him, thereby blocking the keeper or landowner from doing so. On conviction, the fine imposed by the JP was required by law to go to the informant, who would hand it back to the poacher in return for a drink.

The songs in this section display a corresponding mixture of caution, penitence and bravado. They link up with transportation ballads, because by the early nineteenth century seven or fourteen years' transportation had become the standard penalty for poaching. Following the repeal of the Black Act, a succession of laws brought in less draconic penalties, partly at least in recognition of the reluctance of juries to convict:

the Night Poaching Act of 1828 set a maximum term of seven years' imprisonment (or fourteen years for offenders armed with guns), and the Poaching Prevention Act of 1862 allowed fines to be imposed on suspiciously equipped individuals. It is probable that this legal downscaling accounts for the transition from the sense of doom in the older poaching ballads like 'Johnnie of Cockerslee' to the levity with which the risk of being caught is treated in more recent songs like 'Shooting Goschen's Cocks Up'.

JOHNNIE OF COCKERSLEE

Johnnie rose in a May morning
Called for water to wash his hands
Says, 'Loose to me my good grey dogs
That lie bound in iron bands
That lie bound in iron bands.

'Ye'll busk, ye'll busk my noble dogs
Ye'll busk and mak them bound
For I'm awa to the Broadspear Hill
To ding the dun deer down.'

When Johnnie's mither heard of this
Her hands with dule she wrang
Saying, 'Johnnie for my benison
To the greenwood dinna gang

'Enough ye hae o' the gude wheat-bread
And enough o' the blude-red wine
Sae Johnnie for nae venison
I pray ye stir from hame.'

But Johnnie has buskit his good bend-bow
And his arrows one by one
And he's awa to the Broadspear Hill
To ding the dun deer down

He's lookit east, he's lookit west
And a little below the sun
And there he's spied the dun deer lain
Aneath a bush of broom

Johnnie shot, the dun deer lapt
He had wounded her in the side
And atween the wan water and the wood
His hounds they laid her pride

They ate sae mickle of the venison
And drank sae mickle of the blood
That Johnnie and his twa grey hounds
Fell asleep as if they were dead

Then it's by there cam a stane-auld man
And an ill death may he die
And he's awa to the foresters
As fast as he can flee

What news, what news, ye stane-auld man
What news bring you to me?
Nae news, nae news, ye foresters
But what my eyes did see

As I cam down by Durisdeer
And down amang the scroggs
The bonniest chiel that e'er I saw
Lay sleeping amang his dogs

The sark that was upon his back
Was of the cambric fine
The doublet that was over it
Was of the Lincoln twine

Then out and spak the first forester
The heid man o' them a'
'If this be Johnnie of Cockerslee
Nae nearer will we draw.'

But it's out and spak the sixth forester
His sister's son was he
'If this be Johnnie of Cockerslee
We soon shall gar him die.'

He's set his back against an aik
His foot against a stane
And he has slain the foresters
Has killed them a' but ane

He's brak three ribs in that ane's side
And brak his collar bane
And laid him twa-fold o'er his steed
To carry the tidings hame

They've made them rods o' the hazel bush
And ithers o' the slae-thorn tree
And mony, mony were the men
At the hunting o' Johnnie

Now Johnnie's good bend-bow is broke
And his great grey dogs are slain
And his body lies in Durisdeer
And his hunting it is done.

THE VILLAGE OF Durisdeer is in Dumfries, to the south of the Lowther Hills. Local tradition at one time associated a ruined tower near Lochmaben, known as Cockiesfield, with a renowned freebooter known as John Cock.

This version of one of the great border ballads ends in Johnnie's death; but the narrative is sometimes configured so that, in place of the four final stanzas given here, it ends heroically:

Johnnie's killed the six o' them
And the seventh he's wounded sair
And he's swung his leg o'er his horse's back
And swore that he would hunt mair.

The present text is collated from Kinloch's manuscript, printed by Child, and Scott's *Minstrelsy* (a source requiring some caution). The tune, printed by Bronson, is from the Duncan manuscript, taken down from Alexander Mackay of Alford, who had learned it circa 1860.

busk: get ready
ding: strike
dule: anguish
benison: blessing

stane-auld: ancient
scroggs: low bushes
chiel: youth
gar: make

CHILD #114   ROUD #69

SHOOTING GOSCHEN'S COCKS UP

Come listen to me for a while, a story I will tell you
If you won't pay attention then I'm sure I can't compel
     you
You've asked me for to sing and so I'd better start at
     once
I'll tell you how I got six weeks and my mate got two
     months

> *With my row dow dow*
> *Fol de riddle addy*
> *With my row dow dow*

It was on a Monday night that myself, two mates
     and Clarky
We went a-pheasant shooting in a place we knew
     was narky

Five keepers rushed upon us and the guns began to rattle
It caused our mates to do a bunk and left us to the battle

Now me and Clarke was captured and taken to the
    lockup
We was charged before the magistrates for shooting
    Goschen's cocks up
If our mates had not run away we'd never have been
    taken
But all we got to think of was our wives and little children

They put us in the cells, my boys, they got us grinding
    flour
Likewise a-pumping water, boys, unto some lofty tower.
But now I've got this glass of beer it's making me feel
    merry –
My mate he don't get out of gaol till the middle of
    Jan-u-ary.

THE VICTORIAN STATESMAN Lord Goschen (1831–1907) had
a large estate at Seacox Heath on the Sussex-Kent border. For
a poacher towards the end of the nineteenth century, attempt-
ing to bag some of Goschen's well-fed cock pheasants might
have been worth a couple of months in gaol. Even with hard
labour on the treadwheel or treadmill (which was introduced
in 1818 and not abandoned until after 1898 when the reforming
Prison Act was passed) it was a far cry from transportation.

This song has some of the hallmarks of a single author –
neat rhymes, tidy rhythms and (in the version sung by Pop

Maynard of Copthorne, Sussex) a good deal of detail about the procedure of the local magistrates and the prison warders. Maynard in fact thought it had been composed by his friend Fred Holman, who wrote out the words for him in return for a pint.

The present version (subject to some reassembly) was recorded in 1966 from Joe Saunders on Biggin Hill in Kent. The refrain is traced by Chappell to a melody popular in the eighteenth century and known as 'Bow Wow Wow' or 'The Barking Barber'.

ROUD #902

THE LINCOLNSHIRE POACHER

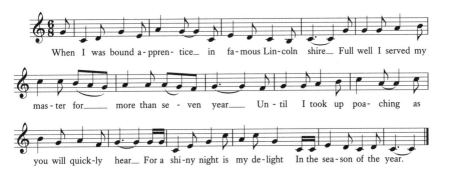

When I was bound apprentice in famous Lincolnshire
Full well I served my master for more than seven year
Until I took up poaching as you shall quickly hear
    For a shiny night is my delight
    In the season of the year.

As me and my companions were setting of a snare
A gamekeeper was watching us, for him we did not care
For we can wrestle and fight, my boys, and jump out
        anywhere
    And a shiny night is my delight
    In the season of the year.

As me and my companions were setting four or five
A-taking of them up again we catched the hare alive
We threw her on our shoulders and through the woods
        did steer
    For a shiny night is my delight
    In the season of the year.

We threw her on our shoulders and wandered through
the town
We called into an alehouse and sold her for a crown
We sold her for a crown, my boys, I will not tell you
where
For a shiny night is my delight
In the season of the year.

Now here's success to poaching, for I do think it fair
Bad luck to every gamekeeper that will not sell
his deer
Good luck to every gentleman that wants to buy a hare
For a shiny night is my delight
In the season of the year.

THIS TEXT OF a song widespread in England was taken down
by Alfred Williams in 1916 from William Bradshaw of Bibury,
Gloucestershire.

Bell's *Ballads and Songs* (1857) gives a bolder final verse:

Bad luck to every magistrate that lives in Lincolnshire
Success to every poacher that wants to sell a hare
Back luck to every gamekeeper that will not sell his
deer . . .

The song appears on a York broadside as early as 1776, but
the *New Penguin Book of English Folk Songs*, pp. 502–3, gives
grounds for believing it was rewritten and popularized as a
stage song in the mid-nineteenth century.

The melody is pretty constant, but the distinctive refrain given here comes from Joe Saunders (see above), recorded in 1966.

'I'll sing you one they larns 'em in the school,' said Joe, 'Only they don't larn it 'em right.'

ROUD #299

THE OAKHAM POACHERS

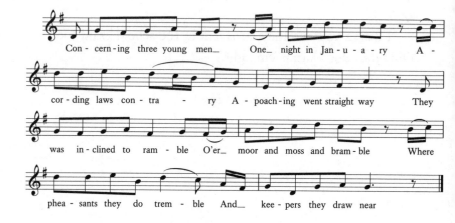

Con - cern - ing three young men— One— night in Jan - u - a - ry   A -
cor - ding laws con - tra - ry   A - poach - ing went straight way   They
was in - clined to ram - ble   O'er— moor and moss and bram - ble   Where
phea - sants they do trem - ble   And— kee - pers they draw near

Concerning of three young men
One night in January
According laws contrary
A-poaching went straightway
They was inclined to ramble
O'er moor and moss and bramble
Where pheasants they do tremble
And keepers they draw near

Oh the keepers dared not enter
Nor cared those woods to venture
But outside round their centre
All in them bush they lay
Oh these poachers soon grew tired
To leave they soon desired
But then young Parkins fired
And he spilled one keeper's blood

He on the ground lay dying
And in his blood there lying
And no assistance nigh him
To see him where he lay
And as they were leaving
And homeward they were speeding
The other keeper stealing
They fired at him also

Oh he on the ground lay bleeding
And for his life there pleading
While through the woods come speeding
His mournful pity cry
They taken were with speed
All for that inhuman deed
For them there was no reprieve
All in the court next day

Oh the judge and the jury tried us
And we for pity cried us
Oh mercy don't deny us
We're not prepared to die
Oh the jury they consulted
Some said we should be gaoled
And others said transported
But the judge said we must die

Oh it never happened before
Two brothers hanged together

Two brothers hanged together
For doing of one crime.

THIS TRAGIC BALLAD, also known as 'The Bold Poachers', does not necessarily belong to the period when poaching was capable of being a capital felony. Whichever of the brothers fired the fatal shots, the judge would have ruled that they were engaged in a joint enterprise and were both guilty of murdering the gamekeepers.

It has not been possible, however, to tie this particular narrative, involving the hanging of two young brothers, to a historical event. It may relate to the trial and conviction in 1833 of three brothers, John, Robert and George Perkins, who had badly wounded a gamekeeper, Thomas Peach:

He on the ground lay crying
Like one that was a-dying
And no assistance nigh him . . .

But Peach survived to give evidence against them. All three were convicted and condemned to death, presumably under the Game Laws. John was hanged; the sentences on Robert and George were commuted to transportation for life.

Tending to confirm this history, the text has phrases suggesting a broadside origin, and the song is listed in a number of nineteenth-century broadside printers' catalogues. Its tune, too, suggests the chapman's intonation described by Mayhew and others. An oral version of it was collected in 1921 from Robert Miller of Sutton, Norfolk, by Edward Moeran.

The song is taken here from Martin Carthy's repertoire. It is a song, Martin has written, which 'proves for me the truth of the maxim that it's not what a song says, necessarily, but what it does that counts'

ROUD #1686

THORNYMOOR WOODS

In Thornymoor Woods in Nottinghamshire
Fol de rol laddie, right fol laddie dee
In Thornymoor Woods in Nottinghamshire
Fol de rol laddie dee
Three keepers' houses stood three-square
About a mile from each other they were
Their orders were to look after the deer
Fol de rol laddie aye day

I went out with my dogs one night
The moon shone clear and the stars gave light
Over hedges and ditches, gates and rails
With my two dogs running close at my heels
To catch a fine buck in Thornymoor fields

But oh, that night we had bad luck
One of my very best dogs was stuck
He came to me both bleeding and lame
Right sorry was I to see the same
For he wasn't able to follow the game

I searched his wounds and found them slight
Some keeper has done this out of spite
But I'll take my pikestaff, that's the plan
I'll range the woods till I find the man
And I'll tan his hide right well if I can

I ranged the woods and groves all night
I ranged the woods till it proved daylight
And the very first thing that then I found
Was a good fat buck laid dead on the ground
I knew my dogs had gave him his death-wound

We hired a butcher to skin the game
Likewise another to sell the same
But the very first buck he offered for sale
Was to an old whore who sold bad ale
She had us three lads sent to Nottingham Gaol

But the quarter sessions was drawing near
At which we all were to appear
The chairman laughed the matter to scorn
He said the old woman was all forsworn
And into little pieces torn

The sessions are over and we are clear
The sessions are over and we sit here
The very best game I ever did see
Is a buck or a deer or a hare for me
And in Thornymoor Woods this night
    we'll be.

JAMES DIXON, in *Ancient Poems, Ballads and Songs*, located this narrative in the manor of Thornehagh or Thornymoor in Northamptonshire, where 800 acres of common land had been enclosed by the Nevile family in 1797.

Like other poaching ballads, this song demonstrates some familiarity with the legal process. While assizes would be presided over by a high court judge sitting with a jury of local property-owners, the quarter sessions, which since 1363 had been required to sit four times a year, and which from 1842 tried the less grave cases, consisted of local justices of the peace.

In some variants the poachers are tried at the assizes, but in this version it is the chairman of the sessions who has evidently taken against the old woman. If so, it may have been because many prosecutions, in the absence of a local constabulary, depended on the evidence of paid informers.

The song is found both on printed broadsides and in oral tradition. This version is based on Dixon's text, collated with a broadside from Kendrew's press in York, circa 1820.

Of several fine tunes found with it, the one used here was collected in 1921 by Cecil Sharp from Kathleen Williams at Puddlebrook in Herefordshire.

There is further information on the song in the notes to #142 in the *New Penguin Book of English Folksongs*.

stuck: see the introductory note on dog-spears
forsworn: perjured

ROUD #222

THE GALLANT POACHERS

Come all you lads of high renown
Who love to drink strong ale that's brown
And bring the lofty pheasant down
With powder, shot and gun

I and five more a-poaching went
To kill some game was our intent
Our money being gone and spent
We'd nothing else to try

The moon shone bright, not a cloud in sight
The keeper heard us fire a gun
And swore before the rising sun
That one of us must die

The bravest youth among the lot
'Twas his misfortune to be shot
His deeds shall never be forgot
By all his friends below

It was the wound that the keeper gave
No mortal man his life could save

He now lies sleeping in his grave
Until the judgment day

To prison then we all were sent
We called for aid but none was lent
Our enemies they were full bent
That there we should remain

But fortune unto us proved kind
And unto us did change her mind
With heartfelt thanks for liberty
We were let out again

No more locked up in midnight cells
To hear the turnkeys ring the bells
Those cruckling doors I bid farewell
And rattling of the chains.

EARLY RELEASE, such as the song recounts, was rare except by the grant of a royal pardon. If the surviving poachers here were spared gaol or released early, it may have been because of the unlawful killing of their comrade by the gamekeeper.

The song, common on broadsides from the 1820s, is closely related to a Luddite song which begins:

Come cropper lads of high renown
Who love to drink strong ale that's brown
And strike each haughty tyrant down
With hatchet, pike and gun

It is not certain, in fact, which song came first.

The tune is the first strain of the version of the poaching song given to Roy Palmer by Walter Pardon of Knapton, Norfolk. It had come to him from his grandfather Tom Gee.

The words are found on nineteenth-century broadsides. The earliest probably came from the press of James Catnach, who was printing in Monmouth Court, Seven Dials, between 1813 and 1838.

Cruckling: probably a corruption of 'clanking',
but too good to edit out

ROUD #793

AFFRAY AND RIOT

Crimes of group violence fell – as they still technically do – into two classes: causing alarm and fear in bystanders, and using force to achieve an unlawful objective. The first is known as affray, from the Norman-French *effroi*, meaning fear. The second, chronicled in a good many ballads and songs, is riot.

Although riot was criminalized for centuries by the common law wherever three or more persons assembled with violent intent, the Restoration parliament in 1661 made it a statutory riot for more than ten persons to assemble in order to present a petition to the sovereign; and in 1817 (in the turbulent period following the defeat of Napoleon) the Seditious Meetings Act made it a riot for more than fifty persons to assemble in the Westminster area while Parliament was sitting.

A century earlier, the Riot Act of 1715, which lived on well into the twentieth century, required local officials to disperse by proclamation, and if need be by force, any riotous gathering of twelve or more persons – hence the expression 'reading the Riot Act'. Until the nineteenth century, the gallows often awaited rioters who were apprehended. Local justices also had a common-law power and duty (notoriously abused in 1819 at

St Peter's Field, Manchester – the Peterloo massacre) to use armed force if necessary to suppress riots.

Ballad tradition is less interested in such details than in the events surrounding them and in their dramatic aftermath. Unsurprisingly, it is the great northern ballads which are richest in these narratives, from the cowardly gang-killing of the ploughboy lover in 'The Dowie Dens of Yarrow' to the two-day pitched battle fought in August 1388 between the Douglas and Percy clans over hunting rights in the Cheviot Hills. The latter of these events, the Battle of Otterburn, is recounted in the great narrative ballad known as 'Chevy Chase' or 'The Hunting of the Cheviot', an epic which it has not been feasible to reduce to manageable proportions for this book but which contains some superb alliterative verse:

> The drivers through the woodes went
> For to raise the deer
> Bowmen bickered [=shot] upon the bent [=fields]
> With their broad arrows clear
>
> The wild [=game] through the woodes went
> On every sidë sheer
> Greyhounds through the grevis [=groves] glent [=darted]
> For to kill their deer

'I must confesse my own barbarousness,' wrote Sir Philip Sidney in 1580, 'I never heard the old song of *Percy and Duglas* that I found not my heart moved more than with a Trumpet; and yet it is sung by some old blind Crouder, with no rougher voice than rude style . . .'

THE BARON OF BRACKLEY (INVEREY)

Down Dee-side cam_ In - ver - ey_ whist-ling and_ play-ing He's ligh - ted at_ Brack-ley's yett_ ere the day's_ daw - ing Say-ing, 'Ba - ron o'_ Brack-ley, O are ye with - in?_____ There's sharp swords at_ your_ yett shall_ gar your bluid rin.'

Down Deeside cam Inverey whistling and playing
He's lighted at Brackley's yett ere the day's dawing
Saying, 'Baron o' Brackley, o are ye within?
There's sharp swords at your yett shall gar your bluid rin.'

His lady raise up, tae the window she went
She heard the kye lowing o'er hill and o'er bent
'Then rise up my baron and turn back your kye
For the lads frae Drumwharren are driving them by.'

'Come tae yer bed Peggy and let the kye rin
For were I tae gang out I wad never come in.'
'Gin I had a husband whereas I hae nane
He wadna lie in his bed and see his kye ta'en.'

'Then kiss me my Peggy, I'll nae langer stay
For I will go out and I'll meet Inverey.'

There was thirty with Inverey, thirty and three
There was nane wi' the baron but his brother and he

Wi' swords and wi' daggers they did him surround
They've pierced bonny Brackley wi' mony a wound
Frae the head of the Dee to the banks of the Spey
The Gordons may mourn him and curse Inverey

O cam ye by Brackley and was ye in there
And saw ye his Peggy a-riving her hair?
O I cam by Brackley and I was in there
And I saw his Peggy a-braiding her hair

She was ranting and dancing and singing for joy
And vowing that nicht she would feast Inverey
She's ate with him, drank with him, welcomed him in
She was kind to the villain who had slain her guid man

There's dule in the kitchen but mirth in the ha'
For the Baron o' Brackley is dead and awa'
But up spak the son upon his nourrice' knee
''Gin I live to be a man, revengèd I'll be.'

IN SEPTEMBER 1666, John Farquharson of Inverey came with armed men to reclaim some cattle which John Gordon, the laird of Brackley, had impounded. Inverey took the opportunity not only to retrieve his own cattle but to steal some of Gordon's, forcing Gordon to come out and enabling Inverey's men to kill him. This, at least, was the Gordons' account, on which the ballad is founded.

The Inverey family some years later gave a different account: Brackley had seized some of their cattle as surety for a fine (either for killing blackfish or for taking salmon out of season from the Dee) which Brackley had bought from the sheriff of Aberdeen. Inverey, who happened to be captain of the watch, had come to settle the fine, but Brackley treated him with contempt, assembled a posse and attacked him and his men, resulting in three deaths on each side.

The one element of the ballad for which there is no evidence at all is that Brackley was driven by his wife's taunts into the fatal confrontation, and that after his death she made Inverey welcome. Brackley's wife Margaret Burnet (Peggy in the ballad) had married him for love against her family's wishes.

Brackley is near Ballater, on the Dee, some forty miles west of Aberdeen. In 1592, an earlier baron of Brackley had been killed in a raid mounted by the Clanchattan against the Huntlys to avenge the killing of the Earl of Murray.

The present text combines elements of Child's three principal sources, Jamieson, Skene and Kinloch. The tune was recorded in 1954 from Anne Neilson of Glasgow by Norman Buchan for the School of Scottish Studies.

yett: gate	**riving:** tearing
kye: cattle	**dule:** grief
bent: meadow	**nourrice:** nurse

CHILD #203   ROUD #401

THE BATTLE OF HARLAW

Down Dee - side cam_ In - ver - ey_ whist - ling and_ play - ing He's
ligh - ted at_ Brack - ley's yett_ ere the day's_ daw - ing Say - ing,
'Ba - ron o'_ Brack - ley, O are ye with - in?_ There's
sharp swords at_ your_ yett shall_ gar your bluid rin.'

As I cam in by Dunidier
And doun by Netherha'
There was fifty thousand Hieland men
A-marching to Harlaw

Wi' a dree-dree-dradie
Drum-tie dree

As I cam in and farther on
And doun by Balquhain
It's there I met Sir James the Rose
Wi' him Sir John the Graeme

'Oh cam ye frae the Hielands, man
And cam ye a' the way
Saw ye Macdonell and his men
As they cam frae the Skee?'

'Yes me cam frae the Hielands, man
And me cam a' ta way
An' she saw Macdonell and his men
As they came frae the Skee.'

'Oh was ye near Macdonell's men
Did ye their numbers see?
Come tell to me John Hielandman
What micht their numbers be.'

'Yes I was near and near eneuch
An' me their numbers saw
There was fifty thousand Hielandmen
A-marching to Harlaw.'

'Gin that be true,' says James the Rose
'We'll no come meikle speed
We'll cry upon our merry men
And lichtly mount our steed.'

'O no, o no,' says John the Graeme
'That thing maun never be
The gallant Graemes were never bate
We'll try what we can dee

'The Hielandmen wi' their lang swords
They laid on us fu' sair
And they drave back our merry men
Three acres breadth and mair

'Macdonell he was young and stout
Had on his coat o' mail
And he has gane out thro' them a'
To try his hand himsel'

'The first ae straik that Forbës struck
He gart Macdonell reel
The neist ae straik that Forbës struck
The great Macdonell fell

'And siccan a lierachie
I'm sure ye never saw
As was amang the Hielandmen
When they saw Macdonell fa'

'They rade, they ran, and some did gang
They were o' sma' record
But Forbës and his merry men
They slew them a' the road

'On Monanday at morning
The battle it begun
On Saturday at gloaming
Ye'd scarce ken wha had won.'

IN JULY 1411, Donald of the Isles, to stake the Clan Macdonell's
(probably legitimate) claim to the earldom of Ross, invaded
the mainland with ten thousand islanders and men of Ross.
Aiming to sack Aberdeen, Macdonell had reached the Tay

when he was met and defeated at Harlaw, eighteen miles from his objective, by an army raised by the Earl of Mar and the sheriff of Angus. The Lowlanders lost about five hundred men; the invaders almost twice that. This was a massive disturbance that without doubt constituted a riot (also known in Scots law as mobbing) but which no civil power could have halted.

The full version of the ballad, communicated to Child in 1888 by an informant who had learnt it from 'the country people' half a century before, is of unmanageable length and has been reduced here. The use of 'me' and 'she' for 'I' in the fourth and sixth verses, while probably used here mockingly, was authentic Highland speech.

The tune was given to Gavin Greig in 1906 by J. W. Spence of Fyvie.

bate: beaten

siccen a lierachie: such disorder

(from 'leerach', the lining of a dungpit)

CHILD #163   ROUD #2861

THE DOWIE DENS OF YARROW

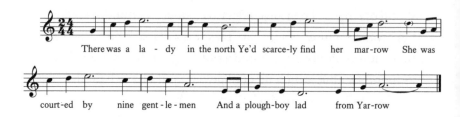

There was a lady in the north
Ye'd scarcely find her marrow
She was courted by nine gentlemen
And a ploughboy lad from Yarrow

These nine sat drinking at the wine
Sat drinking wine in Yarrow
And they made a vow among themselves
To fight for her on Yarrow

She's washed his face, she's kamed his hair
As oft she'd done before O
She's made him like a knight sae bright
Tae fecht for her on Yarrow

As he went up yon high high hill
And down the glen sae narrow
It's there he saw nine armèd men
Come tae fecht wi' him on Yarrow

It's three he's wounded, three withdrew
And three he's killed on Yarrow

Then her brither steppèd in behind
And pierced his body thorough

'O father dear, I dreamed a dream
I fear it will bring sorrow
I dreamed I was pulling heather green
On the dowie dens of Yarrow.'

'O daughter dear, I read your dream
I fear it will bring sorrow
Your true love John lies pale and wan
On the dowie dens of Yarrow.'

As she went up the high high hill
And down the glen sae narrow
It's there she found her true love John
On the dowie dens of Yarrow

She's washed his face, she's kamed his hair
As oft she'd done before O
She's kissed the blood from off his wounds
On the dowie dens of Yarrow

Her hair it was three quarters long
The colour it was yellow
She's wrapped it round his middle sma'
And carried him hame frae Yarrow

'O father dear, ye've seven sons
Ye could wed them a' tomorrow

> But a fairer flower ye never saw
> Than the lad I loved on Yarrow.'

YARROW IS THE name of a loch (Yarrow Water), a river (a tributary of the Tweed) and a parish in the Borders.

Although the ballad features in Child's collection, the finest sets of it were collected or published after his fourth volume went to press in 1890. The present version is collated from Child, Greig, a variant collected by Peggy Seeger and Ewan MacColl in 1962 from Jock Higgins, a Traveller, of Blairgowrie, Perthshire, and the version published in Frank Kidson's *Traditional Tunes*, sung to Kidson by a Mrs Calvert of Gilnockie, Eskdale, who had learnt it from her grandmother Tibbie Shiel.

The tune, collected in 1907 by Lucy Broadwood from John Potts of Peeblesshire, is a variant of the principal group of melodies.

marrow: partner or equal
den: valley or glen
dowie: sad

CHILD #214   ROUD #13

HOMICIDE

There is both more and less to murder than deliberately killing another person. The intention may have been to kill someone else, but the killing is still murder. So is killing when the intention is not to kill but to do serious harm. Curiously, the modern European Convention on Human Rights authorizes killing 'when absolutely necessary . . . in order to effect a lawful arrest' – two things which, even in the ballad tradition, seem irreconcilable. Beyond these issues lie such questions as provocation – was the killer goaded beyond what a reasonable person can be expected to endure? – and the mental state which is today classed as diminished responsibility. Then there is killing in self-defence. There is little that is simple about homicide.

Many of these problems turn up in the ballad narratives. The young trooper McCaffery went to the gallows for shooting an officer he had no intention of harming. The Earl of Huntly when he killed the Earl of Murray held a warrant for his arrest. Lord Barnard, not unreasonably, thought Gil Norice was his wife's lover, not her son. Whether the drowning of the outlandish knight, an admitted serial killer, was legitimate self-defence when the maiden could simply have ridden off is probably of more interest to lawyers than to singers.

THE BONNY EARL OF MURRAY

Ye hie-lands and ye low-lands O where hae ye been? They hae slain the Earl of Mur-ray And laid him on the green He was a braw gal-lant And he play-ed at the glove And the bon-ny Earl of Mur-ray Was the queen's ain love Lang may his la-dy Look frae the cas-tle down Till she see the Earl of Mur-ray Come sound-ing through the town

Ye hielands and ye lowlands
O where hae ye been?
They hae slain the Earl of Murray
And laid him on the green
He was a braw gallant
And he played at the glove
And the bonny Earl of Murray
Was the queen's ain love

Lang may his lady
Look frae the castle down

57

Till she see the Earl of Murray
Come sounding through the town

Now woe be tae ye Huntly
And wherefore did ye sae?
I bade ye bring him wi' ye
But forbade ye him to slay
He was a braw gallant
And he rid at the ring
And the bonny Earl of Murray
He might have been a king

Lang may his lady
Look frae the castle down
Till she see the Earl of Murray
Come sounding through the town.

IN FEBRUARY 1592, the Earl of Huntly secured the king's commission to arrest his enemy the Earl of Murray and bring him to trial for abetting the Earl of Bothwell's treasonable activities (in which Huntly himself had been involved). Murray, a Stewart and a famously handsome man, who had obtained the earldom by marrying the Murray heiress, was at his mother's home at Donibristle with almost no retinue. He tried to fight Huntly off, but the house was set on fire and Murray was hunted down as he tried to escape. His body was left unburied in Leith (hence 'laid him on the green'). His friends attempted to get Huntly punished, but the king would not act.

The suggestion in the ballad that Murray 'was the queen's love' probably derives from the rumour that not long before his death the queen had been heard speaking fulsomely of him.

Of the known tunes, the earliest is found in Thomson's *Orpheus Caledonius* (1733), but perhaps the handsomest, used here, was recovered in north America from the singing of an unnamed Scot who in 1906 had learned it from one of the Murray family. Bronson, acknowledging its modern currency, considers it to have 'a mournful beauty' but to be 'not very folklike, or at any rate balladlike'. Not everyone will agree.

CHILD #181   ROUD #334

GIL NORICE

Gil No-rice is tae__ the green-wood gane A - wa' he's with the -
wind His__ horse is__ sil - ler-shod a - fore Wi'__ shin - ing gowd be - hind

Gil Norice is tae the greenwood gane
Awa he's with the wind
His horse is siller-shod afore
Wi' shining gowd behind

He said unto his wee boy John
'I see what ye dinna see
I see the first woman that e'er I loved
Or ever lovèd me.'

'Here is a glove, a glove' he said
'Lined with the silver-gray
Tell her to come to the merry greenwood
To speak wi' Gil Norey.'

'Here is a ring, a ring' he said
'It's a' gold but the stane
Tell her to come to the merry greenwood
And ask the leave o' nane.'

'And tak tae her this sark o' silk
Her ain hand sewed the sleeve

Bid her come tae the gay greenwood
And ask not Barnard's leave.'

'I daurna gang tae Lord Barnard's castle
I daurna for my life
I daurna gang tae Lord Barnard's castle
Tae twine him o' his wife.'

'Do I nae pay ye gowd,' he said
'Do I nae pay you fee?
How dare you stand my bidding,' he said
'When I bid ye tae flee?'

When he came to Lord Barnard's castle
He tirlèd at the ring
And nane sae ready as Lord Barnard
Tae let this wee boy in

'What news, what news, my bonny wee boy
What news hae ye for me?'
'Nae news, nae news Lord Barnard,' he said
'But your lady I fain would see

'Here is a pair of gloves tae her
Lined wi' the silver-gray
Tell her to come to the merry greenwood
And speak to Gil Norey

'And here's a gay gowd ring for her
It's a' gowd but the stane

And she maun come tae the gay greenwood
And ask the leave o' nane

'Here is a gay manteil for her
Her ain hand sewed the sleeve
And she maun come to the gay greenwood
And ask not Barnard's leave.'

Lord Barnard he was standing by
And an angry man was he
'Little did I think there was any man
My lady loved but me.'

Lord Barnard's tae a dressing-room
Busk't him in woman's array
And he's awa tae the gay greenwood
Tae speak wi' Gil Norey.

Gil Norey he stood in guid greenwood
He whistled and he sang:
'I think I see the woman come
That I hae lovèd lang.'

Lord Barnard had a nut-brown sword
That hung down by his knee
And he has cut Gil Norey's head
Off from his fair body

He has ta'en Gil Norey's head
And set it on a spear

The meanest man in a' his train
Has gotten the head to bear

The lady sat on the castle wall
Beheld baith dale and down
And there she saw Gil Norey's head
Come trailing tae the town

She took the bloody head in her hand
And kissed it cheek and chin
Saying, 'Better I like that well-faured face
Than a' my royal kin.

'When I was in my father's bower
In my virginity
There cam a lord into the north
And gat Gil Norice wi' me.

'I got him in my father's bower
Wi' mickle sin and shame
I brought him up in the gay greenwood
Beneath the heavy rain.'

Then out and spak Lord Barnard
And an angry man was he
Saying, 'Had I kent he was your son
He'd ne'er been slain by me.'

THE BALLAD OF GIL (or Child) Noreys (or Norice or Maurice), gathered by Child from several early manuscript sources, is striking not for its naive story but for the beauty of the language in which it is told. The present version, drawing on several of Child's sources, is structured in the classic format – multiple gifts, recounted in detail and enumerated again on delivery, with dreadful consequences. The opening line may be an echo of the fragment sung in feigned madness by Edgar in *King Lear*: 'Child Roland to the dark tower came.'

Faced with the unlikelihood of an unacknowledged love-child turning up with rich gifts on a gold-shod horse, a version of the ballad given to Motherwell in 1826 by a widow, Mrs Michael, who had learnt it in Banffshire seventy years before, contains a final verse which suggests a viable back-story: that Gil Norice's father, the lord who had come 'into', or equally possibly out of, the north, was a Scandinavian nobleman who had taken the boy as an infant and brought him up as his heir:

> Keep weel your land, [Barnard], she said
> Your land and white monie
> There's land eneuch in Noroway
> Lies heirless I wat the day.

The melody used here was given in 1825 to Motherwell by an informant identified simply as A. Blaikie, Paisley.

siller: silver **gowd:** gold **flee:** fly
stane: stone **weel-faur'd:** well-favoured

CHILD #83   ROUD #53

CLERK SAUNDERS

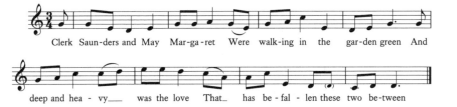

Clerk Saunders and May Margaret
Were walking in the garden green
And deep and heavy was the love
That has befallen these two between

'A bed, a bed,' Clerk Saunders said
'A bed my love for you and me.'
'Fie no, fie no,' the lady said
'Until the day we married be

'For in will come my seven brothers
And all their torches burning bright
They'll say we have but one sister
And here she's lying with you the night.'

'Then I'll take the sword from my scabbard
And slowly slowly lift the pin
And you may swear to save your oath
You never let Clerk Saunders in

You'll take me up into your arms
And lay me low down on your bed

And you may swear to save your oath
That your bower-floor I did not tread.'

They were not well into the room
Nor yet well laid into the bed
When in and cam her seven brothers
And all their torches burning red

Out and spak the first of them
'We will awa and let them be.'
And it's out and spak the second one
'His father has nae mair but he.'

Out and spak the third of them
'I wat they have been lovers dear.'
Out and spak the fourth of them
'They've been in love this many a year.'

Out and spak the fifth of them
'O but their love be wondrous keen.'
And out and spak the sixth of hem
''Twere sin to kill a sleeping man.'

But out and spak the seventh brother
'Although there were no man but me
I bear the brand into my hand
Shall quickly gar Clerk Saunders die.'

And he's ta'en out a rusty brand
And drew it three times through the strae

And through and through Clerk Saunders'
    body
He gart the rusty rapier gae

Clerk Saunders started and Margaret turned
Intae his arms as asleep she lay
And there she slept by her love's side
Until the dawning of the day

'Awake awake Clerk Saunders,' she said
'Awake awake for sin and shame
 For the sheets they are asweat,' she said
'And I'm afraid we shall be ta'en.'

But he lay still and sleepèd sound
Albeit the sun began to shine
She looked between her and the wa'
And dull and heavy were his e'en

'O woe be unto my brother
I wat an ill death may he die
He's killed Clerk Saunders, an earl's son
That pledged his faith to marry me.'

THE TEXT RECORDED by Kinloch (1827) has an almost cine-
matic opening verse:

It was a sad and rainy night
As ever rained from town to town

> Clerk Saunders and his lady gay
> They were in the fields so brown

In longer versions of the ballad, Saunders reappears as a ghost and has to leave at daybreak:

> O cocks are crowing on merry middle-earth
> I wat the wild fowls are boding day

The present text, collated from variants in the Herd MSS, follows what Child considered the essential narrative, striking for its chilling realism when, as day dawns, Margaret realizes that the sheets are wet, not with sweat, but with her lover's blood. The tune is from Motherwell's *Minstrelsy* (1827).

CHILD #69   ROUD #3855

LITTLE MUSGRAVE AND LADY BARNARD

As it fell on one holy day
As many be in the year
Little Musgrave would to the church to pray
And see the fine ladies there

Some came down in red velvet
And some came down in pall
And then came down my lady Barnard
The fairest of them all

She cast a look on little Musgrave
Bright as the summer's sun
And then bethought him little Musgrave
This lady's love I have won

'Good day, good day, you handsome youth
God make you safe and free
What would you give this day, Musgrave
For a night in bower with me?'

'I dare not for my lands, lady
I dare not for my life

For the ring on your white finger shows
You are Lord Barnard's wife.'

'Lord Barnard is a-hunting gone
I hope he'll ne'er return
And you shall sleep into his bed
And keep his lady warm.

'You nothing have to fear, Musgrave
You nothing have to fear
I'll set my page without the gate
To watch till morning clear.'

But woe be to the wee foot-page
An ill death may he die
For he's away to the greenwood
As fast as he can flee

When he came to the wan water
He slacked his bow and swam
And when he came to growing grass
Set down his feet and ran

And when he to the greenwood came
'Twas dark as dark could be
He found his master and his men
Asleep aneath a tree

'Rise up, rise up, master,' he said
'Rise up and speak to me

Your wife's in bed with little Musgrave
Rise up right speedily.'

'If this be true you tell to me
It's gold shall be your fee
If it be false you tell to me
I'll hang you from a tree.'

'Go saddle me the black,' he cried
'Go saddle me the grey
Nor wind no horns,' quoth he, 'on your life
Lest our coming it should betray.'

There was a man in Lord Barnard's train
Had a love to little Musgrave
He blew his horn both loud and high
'Away, Musgrave, away.'

'Methinks I hear the throstle cock
Methinks I hear the jay
Methinks I hear Lord Barnard's horn
"Away, Musgrave, away."'

'Lie still, lie still, thou little Musgrave
And huddle me from the cold
'Tis nothing but a shepherd's boy
Driving his flock to the fold.'

'Is not thy hawk upon the perch
Thy steed eats oats and hay

And thou, a gay lady in thy arms
And yet thou wouldst away.'

He turned him right and round about
And he fell fast asleep
And when he woke Lord Barnard's men
Were standing at his feet

'How do you like my bed, Musgrave
And how like you my sheets
And how like you my lady fair
Lies in your arms and sleeps?'

'It's very well I like your bed
It's well I like your sheets
But foul may fall your lady fair
Lies in my arms and sleeps.'

'Get up get up, young man,' he said
'Get up as swift's you can
It never shall be said in my country
I slew a naked man

'I have two swords in my scabbard
Full dear they cost my purse
And thou shalt have the better one
And I shall have the worse.'

Then slowly slowly rose he up
And slowly put he on

And slowly down the stair he goes
And thinking to be slain

The first stroke little Musgrave got
It was both deep and sair
And down he fell at Barnard's feet
And word spak never mair

'O how d'you like his cheeks, lady
And how d'you like his chin
And how d'you like his fair body
That there's no life within?'

'O well I like his cheeks,' she said
'And well I like his chin
And better I like his fair body
Than all your kith and kin.'

He's taken out a long long brand
And stripped it through the strae
And through and through his lady's sides
He garred the cold steel gae.

THIS IS AS MUCH a drama of character as of events. With Musgrave's less than devout reason for going to church and his unexpected luck in catching Lady Barnard's eye, the liaison is set on a disaster course.

Although neither English nor Scots law has historically recognized 'honour' killing as a defence to murder, Scots law has controversially allowed sexual infidelity to found a defence of provocation, reducing murder to culpable homicide.

The melody given here combines the related tunes taken from oral tradition by Chappell and Motherwell. The text draws on the principal variants assembled by Child.

sair: sore **strae:** straw **garred:** made

CHILD #81   ROUD #52

THE OUTLANDISH KNIGHT

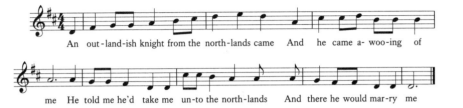

An out-land-ish knight from the north-lands came And he came a- woo-ing of me He told me he'd take me un-to the north-lands And there he would mar-ry me

An outlandish knight came from the northlands
And he came a-wooing of me
He told me he'd take me unto the northlands
And there he would marry me

'Come fetch me some of your father's gold
And some of your mother's fee
And two of the best steeds out of the stable
Where they stand thirty and three.'

She's mounted her on a milk-white steed
Him on a dapple-grey
They rode till they came unto the sea shore
Three hours before it was day

'Light off, light off thy milk-white steed
And deliver it unto me
Six pretty maids have I drownèd here
And thou the seventh shall be

'Take off, take off thy silken gown
And deliver it unto me

Methinks it looks too rich and too gay
To rot in the salt salt sea

'Take off, take off thy silken stays
And deliver them unto me
Methinks they are too fine and gay
To rot in the salt salt sea

'Take off, take off thy holland smock
And deliver it unto me
Methinks it looks too rich and gay
To rot in the salt salt sea.'

'If I must pull off my Holland smock
Pray turn thy back to me
For it is not fitting that such a ruffian
A naked woman should see.'

He turned his back towards her
And viewed the leaves so green
She catched him round the middle small
And tumbled him into the stream

'Lie there, lie there you false-hearted man
Lie there instead of me
Six pretty maids have you drownèd here
And the seventh hath drownèd thee.'

She mounted on her milk-white steed
And led the dapple-grey

She rode till she came to her father's hall
Three hours before it was day

The parrot in the window so high
Hearing the maiden, did say
'O what have you done with the outlandish knight?
You have tarried so long away.'

'Don't prittle, don't prattle, my pretty polly
Nor tell no tales of me
And thy cage shall be made of the glittering gold
And the door of the best ivory.'

Her father being in the chamber so high
And hearing the parrot, did say
'What ails you, what ails you, my pretty parrot
That you prattle so long before day?'

'O master, o master,' replied the parrot
'It's no laughing matter,' said he
'For the cat has got into the window so high
And I fear it will soon have me.'

'Well turnèd, well turnèd my pretty poll parrot
Well turnèd, well turnèd for me
Now thy cage shall be made of the glittering gold
And the door of the best ivory.'

THERE IS A DREAMLIKE quality to the narrative. No time appears to have passed between the pair's departure and the maiden's return: both of them occur 'three hours before it was day'. Given the intervention of the crafty parrot, it is possible that the entire brush with death never occurred.

The tune used here was 'obtained in the North Riding of Yorkshire' by Frank Kidson and published in his supplement to William Chappell's *Old English Popular Music*. Although Dixon in 1846 had written, 'The tune to *The Outlandish Knight* has never been printed; it is peculiar to the ballad, and, from its popularity, is well known,' a variety of tunes have been collected since then with the ballad.

The present text is based on the one published by Dixon in 1846 as 'the common English stall copy of a ballad of which there are variety of versions'. Many of these were assembled by Child, commonly shifting after the first verse, as here, from a first-person to a third-person narrative.

outlandish: according to Dixon, 'By the term "outlandish" is signified an inhabitant of that portion of the border which was formerly known as "the Debateable Land", a district which, though claimed by England and Scotland, could not be said to belong to either country.'
small: slender

CHILD #4   ROUD #21

MCCAFFERY

When I was scarce-ly eight-een years of age To join the ar-my I did en-gage I

left the fact-o-ry with full in-tent To join the Thir-ty sec-ond Reg-i-ment I

left the fact-o-ry with full in-tent To join the Thir-ty Sec-ond Re-gi-ment

When I was scarcely eighteen years of age
To join the army I did engage
I left the factory with full intent
To join the Forty-second Regiment

I left the factory with full intent
To join the Thirty-second Regiment

To Fulwood barracks I then did go
To serve a period in that depòt
But out of trouble I could not be
For Captain Hanson took a dislike to me

While out on sentry-go one day
Some soldiers' children came out to play
I took one's name but not all three
And with neglect of my duty they did charge me

In the barrack courtroom I did appear
But Captain Hanson my story would not hear
My sentence it was quickly signed
And to Fulwood barracks I was confined

For fourteen weeks and thirteen days
My sentence rose and turned my brain
To shoot my captain dead on sight
Was all that I resolved to do each night

I saw him standing on the barrack square
Walking arm in arm with Colonel Blair
I raised my rifle and fired to kill
And shot my poor colonel against my will

I did the deed, I shed the blood
At Liverpool assizes my trial I stood
The judge he said 'McCaffery
Prepare yourself for the gallows tree.'

Now all you young fellows be warned by me
Have nothing to do with the British army
For it's army lies and tyranny
That have made a murderer of McCaffery.

IN OCTOBER 1860 Patrick McCaffery, born in Kildare in 1842, left his job in a Stalybridge cotton mill to enlist in the 32nd regiment [*sic*] of foot and was sent for training to Liverpool's Fulwood Barracks. The barracks commandant was Colonel

Hugh Crofton, a veteran of the Crimean War and a respected soldier. His adjutant, Captain John Hanham, who had been wounded in India, was reputed to be a bully.

On 13 September 1861 McCaffery was required to take some children's names. He did it idly or inefficiently and was put on a charge by Hanham. Colonel Crofton found him guilty and sentenced him to be confined to barracks for fourteen days. Later the same morning McCaffery saw the two officers walking together. He loaded his rifle and with a single shot killed them both: the bullet first penetrated Crofton's chest, then lodged in Hanham's spine. McCaffery was tried in December at Liverpool assizes, and hanged in public the following month.

Apart from three features this is a typical gallows ballad, with irregular metre and a modest melodic range, designed to be heard in a noisy street. First, however, where gallows ballads typically end with a high-flown moral about disobedience or bad company, this one ends with an attack on army discipline (or in some variants, with a warning to officers to treat their men decently). For this reason it was widely believed to be a military offence to sing it.

Second, the ballad-maker suggests that it was only after almost four months' confinement to barracks that McCaffery took leave of his senses. In reality everything had happened within the space of one morning. This was a spontaneous act of revenge by a trooper who unaccountably had access to a rifle and ammunition while undergoing punishment.

Third, the songmaker has missed the single most dramatic aspect of the story, the killing of two officers with a single bullet. This feature is also of some legal interest. If, as the ballad suggests, McCaffery had taken aim at the captain and had by mischance hit only the colonel, would this have afforded him a defence on the ground that there was no intention to harm the eventual victim? No. In this situation the law introduces what it calls transferred malice: the combination of a lethal act with an intent to kill is enough to constitute murder. In any event, the death of the captain was intended and accomplished. The indictment on which McCaffery was tried must accordingly have contained two distinct counts of murder: the intended killing of Captain Hanham, and the unintended but nonetheless malicious killing of Colonel Crofton.

The present version of the ballad comes in part from the singing of Ewan MacColl and in part (in particular the reprise) from Joe Saunders of Biggin Hill.

ROUD #1148

LORD RANDAL

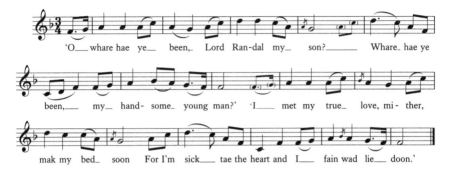

'O___ whare hae ye___ been,__ Lord Ran-dal my___ son?_____ Whare_ hae ye been,____ my__ hand- some_ young man?' 'I___ met my true_ love, mi - ther, mak my bed_ soon For I'm sick___ tae the heart and I___ fain wad lie___ doon.'

'O whare hae ye been, Lord Randal my son?
Whare hae ye been, my handsome young man?'
'I met my true love, mither, mak my bed soon
For I'm sick tae the heart and I fain wad lie doon.'

'What gat ye tae your supper, Lord Randal my son?
What gat ye tae your supper, my handsome young man?'
'Eels in a pan, mither, mak my bed soon
For I'm sick tae the heart and I fain wad lie doon.'

'Wha gat your leavings, Randal my son?
Wha gat your leavings, my bonny young man?'
'My hawk and my hounds, mither, mak my bed soon
For I'm sick tae the heart and I fain wad lie doon.'

'And what becam o' them, Randal my son?
What becam o' them, my handsome young man?'
'They stretched out and died, mither, mak my bed soon
For I'm sick tae the heart and I fain wad lie doon.'

'I fear you are poisoned, Randal my son
If fear you are poisoned, my handsome young man.'
'O yes I am poisoned, mither, mak my bed soon
For I'm sick tae the heart and I fain wad lie doon.'

'What do ye leave your mither, Randal my son?
What do ye leave your mither, my bonny young
      man?'
'Four and twenty milk kye, mither, mak my bed soon
For I'm sick tae the heart and I fain wad lie doon.'

'What do you leave your sister, Randal my son?
What do you leave your sister, my handsome young
      man?'
'My gold and my silver, mither, mak my bed soon
For I'm sick tae the heart and I fain wad lie doon.'

'What d'you leave your brother, Lord Randal my
      son?
What d'you leave your brother, my handsome young
      man?'
'My lands and my houses, mither, mak my bed soon
For I'm sick tae the heart and I fain wad lie doon.'

'What d'ye leave your true love, Lord Randal my
      son?
What d'ye leave your true love, my handsome young
      man?'
'The tow and the halter to hang on yon tree
And let her hang there for the poisoning o' me.'

THE SONG GIVES no clue as to why Randal's lover has poisoned him, but this has not diminished its durability. Burlesque versions of it – most famously 'Enery my son' – became current on the music-hall stage, culminating after the fourth verse in the celebrated line:

Them eels was snakes, Enery my son!

The set given here is a composite of Kinloch's text 'from Mrs Comie, Aberdeen' and the eighteenth-century manuscript copy used by Child as his A text.

Of numerous known tunes, the one used here, from Ayrshire, was given to James Johnson for his *Scots Musical Museum* (1792) by Robert Burns.

CHILD #12   ROUD #10

THE BLIND MAN WHO COULD SEE

'Twas in the town of Kel - so A wo-man she_ did dwell_ She loved her hus-band

dear - ly But a - no -ther man twice as well O -

-fol - de - did - dle ai - ry___ Fol - did-dle ai - ry an

'Twas in the town of Kelso
A woman she did dwell
She loved her husband dearly
But another man twice as well

    O Fol-de-diddle airy
    Foldiddle airy an

She went down to the druggist
Some medicine for to buy
For in her mind she had resolved
Her husband was to die

She bought a pound of marrow-bone
And ground it very small
Before he'd eaten half of it
He couldna see at all

'I'm tired of life,' he cried aloud
'Tired of my life
I think I'll go and drown myself
And that will end the strife.'

Down the street together they went
Till they came to the water's brim
'O will you tak a great lang race
And help tae ding me in.'

And so she took a great lang race
To help to ding him in
But the cunning old bugger he stepped aside
And she went tumbling in

'O save my life, o save me
O help me when I call.'
'How can I come and save you
When I can't see you at all?'

'Now tak ye that, ye auld jade
You thought that I was blind
But I'll gae whistling hame again
And another wife I'll find.'

TRADITIONAL COMIC song is heavily, if not uniformly, miso-gynistic. In this variant of a tale found throughout Ireland, England and Scotland, a dissatisfied wife sets out with murder-ous intent but is outsmarted by her equally murderous husband.

Ground-up marrowbones were evidently believed to cause blindness. The present set is based on a version given to Norman Buchan by George Fraser of Strichen.

ROUD #183

POLLY VAUGHAN

Come all you young sportsmen who carry a gun
I'd have you go home by the light of the sun
Young Jimmy was fowling, a-fowling alone
When he shot his own true love in place of a swan

One midsummer's evening, the sun being gone
Young Polly went walking by the side of a pond
She sat underneath a tree a shower for to shun
With her apron around her as white as a swan

Young Jimmy was a-hunting with his dog and his gun
Young Jimmy was a-hunting as the evening came on
And among the green rushes as the evening came on
He shot his own true love in place of a swan

Then home ran young Jimmy with his dog and his gun
Crying 'Uncle, dear uncle, have you heard what I've done?
Cursed be the old gunsmith who made me this gun
For I've shot my own true love in place of a swan.'

Then up spoke his uncle, his locks growing grey
Saying, 'Jimmy, dear Jimmy, don't you run away
Stay at home my dear Jimmy till the trial do
    come on
For you ne'er will be hangèd for what you have done.'

On the day of his trial young Polly did appear
Saying, 'Uncle, dear uncle, let Jimmy go clear
With my apron wrapped round me he took me
    for a swan
And he shot his own true love in place of a swan.'

THE STORY OF Polly Vaughan (or Molly Bann), riddled with improbabilities and often textually garbled, was dismissed by scholars, despite its wide currency in Britain and Ireland, as (in Jamieson's words) 'a silly ditty, one of the very lowest description of English ballads which are sung about the streets in country towns and sold four or five for a halfpenny' (*Popular Ballads*, 1806). They failed to observe the ballad's relationship to the age-old myth – the basis of *Swan Lake*, among other legends – of the girl who is magically transformed into a swan.

Legally, nevertheless, young Jimmy is in trouble. Throughout the United Kingdom (which from 1801 to 1920 incorporated Ireland) swans were and still are not game. In law they are royal birds, the property of the Crown. Add to this the visual mistake Jimmy claims he made, and even Polly's miraculous reappearance might not have saved him, any more than cursing the gunsmith for his own incompetence as a hunter.

The text given here is assembled from the version sung

by Harry Cox of Yarmouth and variants collected by Sharp, O'Lochlainn and Gardiner, replacing 'in the room of' with 'in place of'.

The tune was collected by Colm O'Lochlainn from Patrick Walsh in the Clogher Valley.

ROUD #166

THE FAMOUS FLOWER OF SERVING-MEN

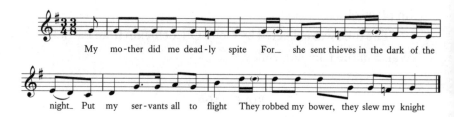

My mother did me deadly spite
For she sent thieves in the dark of the night
Put my servants all to flight
They robbed my bower, they slew my knight

They could do to me no harm
So they slew my baby in my arm
Left me nought to wrap him in
But the bloody sheet that he lay in

They left me nought to dig his grave
But the bloody sword that slew my babe
All alone the grave I made
And all alone the tear I shed

And all alone the bell I rang
And all alone the psalm I sang
I leaned my head all against the block
And there I cut my lovely locks

I cut my locks and I changed my name
From Fair Eleanor to Sweet William

Went to court to serve my king
As the famous flower of serving men

So well I served my lord the king
That he made me his chamberlain
He loved me as his son
The famous flower of serving men

Ofttimes he'd look at me and smile
So swift his heart I did beguile
And he blessed the day that I became
The famous flower of serving men

But all alone in my bed at e'en
It's there I dreamed a dreadful dream
I saw my bed swim with blood
I saw the thieves all around my head

Our king has to the hunting gone
He's ta'en no lords nor gentlemen
He's left me there to guard his home
The famous flower of serving men

Our king he rode the woods all around
Stayed all day but nothing found
And as he rode himself alone
It's there he spied the milk white hind

O the hind she broke, the hind she flew
The hind she trampled the bramble through

First she'd melt and then she'd sound
Sometimes before, sometimes behind

O what is this, how can it be
Such a hind as this I ne'er did see
Such a hind as this was never born
I fear she'll do me deadly harm

And long long did the great horse turn
To save his lord from branch and thorn
Long e'er the day was o'er
They tangled all in his yellow hair

All in a glade the king drew nigh
Where the hind shone so bright in his eye
He sprang down, sword drew
She vanished there all from his view

And all around the grass was green
And all around where a grave was seen
Sat himself down on the stone
Great weariness it seized him on

Great silence hung from tree to sky
The woods grew still, the sun hung fire
As through the wood the dove he came
Through the woods he made his moan

The dove he sat down on a stone
So sweet he looked, so soft he sang

Alas the day my love became
The famous flower of serving men

The bloody tears they fell as rain
Still he sat and still he sang
Alas the day my love became
The famous flower of serving men

Our king cried out and he wept full sore
So loud unto the dove he did call
'Pretty bird come sing it plain
Pretty bird come sing again.'

It was her mother's deadly spite
For she sent thieves in the dark of the night
They come to rob, they come to slay
They made their sport, they went their way

And don't you think her heart was sore
As she laid the mold on his yellow hair
Don't you think her heart was woe
As she turn about all away to go

And how she wept as she changed her name
From Fair Eleanor to Sweet William
Went to court to serve her king
As the famous flower of serving men

The bloody tears they lay all around
He's mounted up and away he's gone

One thought come to his mind
The thought of her that was a man

And as he rode himself alone
A dreadful oath he there has sworn
That he would hunt her mother down
Like he would hunt the wildwood swine

For there's four and twenty ladies all
And they're all playing at the ball
Fairer than all of them
Is the famous flower of serving men

Our king rode in into his hall
He rode in and among them all
Lifted her up his saddle brim
He's kissed her there both cheek and chin

The lords all stood and they stretched their eyes
The ladies hid in their hands and smiled
For a stranger homecoming
No gentleman had ever seen

He has sent his nobles all
To her mother they have gone
Ta'en her that did such wrong
They've lain her down in a prison strong

And he's brought men up from the corn
And he's sent men down to the thorn

For to build the bonfire high
All for to set her mother by

Bonny sang the morning thrush
All where he sat in yonder bush
Louder did her mother cry
In the bonfire where she burned close by

For there she stood all among the thorn
And there she sang her deadly song
Alas the day that she became
The famous flower of serving men

For the fire took first upon her cheek
And there it took all on her chin
Spat and it rang in her yellow hair
As there she burnt like hokey green.

ONE OF THE strangest and most appalling of all the traditional ballads, this lyric abounds in both crime and punishment.

The story in the present version (though not in others) begins with a mother's unexplained destruction of her daughter's home and murder of her child. It moves through a familiar narrative of the girl who passes for a boy until she is recognized and marries her benefactor. And then, hideously, the mother, betrayed by a white hind and a dove, is found and burned alive.

So recounted, the tale could come from the Brothers Grimm or other north European sources; yet Child was able to find no analogues of it. The ballad stands alone not only in this respect but in a diction which is neither that of Anglo-Scots tradition nor that of early English epic verse, suggesting a common broadside origin. The handful of early texts found by Child has been supplemented by a number of oral versions, typically given the title 'Sweet William and Fair Eleanor', collected during the twentieth century in Scotland, southern England and the eastern USA, and all with a happy ending.

Martin Carthy takes up the story:

> There is a whole group of songs and stories in which the heroine, seeking to hide some shame, takes on a disguise . . . In song, one of the forms it has taken is the one known on broadsides as 'The Lady Turned Serving Man', and known in drastically curtailed form to Bishop Percy, Sir Walter Scott and Johnson as 'The Famous Flower of Serving Men' or 'The Lament of the Border Widow'. Having first read 'The Famous Flower' and been fired with enthusiasm, I was sobered by reading the rather pedestrian text of the broadside, which immediately followed, and gave the story an ending, because it simply did not match – either in intensity or elegance – the considerably older, shortened version, and I decided to try and tell it in my own way. The tune came from Hedy West, who sings it to an American song called 'The Maid of Colchester'.

mold: earth
hokey: a fire which has burned down to hot ash; 'hokey green' may signify the blaze when fresh wood is added

CHILD #106   ROUD #199

PIRACY

Piracy is robbery on the high seas. Jurisdiction to try piracy charges is universal. Historically, death by hanging awaited any seaman found guilty of it.

Pirates have since Roman times been regarded by the law of nations as enemies of mankind – *hostes humani generis* – and accordingly subject to summary justice. But this does not mean they had no rights. They could claim the authority of a sovereign or a state, as a number of Elizabethan privateers did. And, unless killed in battle, they were to be tried before the nearest court, as has happened in modern times to Somali fishermen accused of hijacking oil tankers in the Red Sea and delivered to Kenya for trial in Mombasa.

In England and Wales, mariners accused of piracy were tried by the Admiralty Court until 1536, when the Offences at Sea Act made them subject to the process of the common law. To those convicted mercy was rarely shown, especially since the common law regarded British subjects convicted of piracy as guilty of treason.

With the outlawing of the Atlantic slave trade (by Britain in 1807, the USA in 1808 and the principal European powers in

1815), slavers became assimilated to pirates. The last American slave-trader, Captain Nathaniel Gordon, was tried and hanged for piracy in New York in 1862.

A fair amount is known about conditions aboard pirate vessels. At a time when service on both naval and merchant ships was characterized by dangerous conditions, bad pay and almost limitless brutality, articles such as those signed by Bartholomew Roberts's crew gave every man an equal share of the vessel's loot (the captain and quartermaster got double shares); fighting and gaming for money were banned; smuggling women or boys aboard was a capital offence; 'quarrels to be ended on shore at sword and pistol'. There was free access to the ship's victuals unless the crew voted to ration them on account of scarcity. The ship's company was indissoluble until £1,000 per man had been shared out, but until that point was reached desertion was punished by death or marooning. Lights-out was at 8 p.m., after which any drinking was to be done on deck. Not only was there provision in the ship's articles for disability benefit, but the musicians in the ship's orchestra were entitled to Sundays off. Piracy had its attractions.

THE FLYING CLOUD

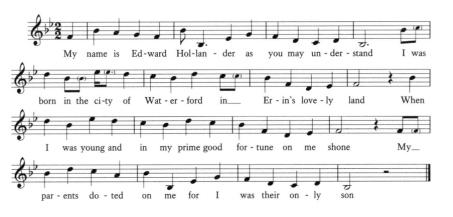

My name is Edward Hollander as you may understand
I was born in the city of Waterford in Erin's lovely
    land
When I was young and in my prime good fortune on
    me shone
My parents doted on me for I was their only son

My father bound me to a trade in Waterford's fair town
He bound me as a butcher boy to a man named
    William Brown
I wore the bloody apron there for three long years
    or more
Then I shipped aboard the *Ocean Queen*, the pride of
    old Tramore

It was on Bermuda's sunny isle I met with Captain
    Moore
The master of the *Flying Cloud* hailing from Baltimore

He offered me good wages if with him I would go
On a slaving voyage to Africa where the sugar cane
do grow

O all went well until we came to Africa's burning
shore
Five hundred of them poor slaves from their native
land we bore
Each one was loaded down with chains and made
to march below
Just eighteen inches to a man was all they had
to show

The plague it came and fever too and swept them off
like flies
We hauled the bodies up on deck and hove them in
the tide
'Twas better for the rest of them if they'd have died
before
Than drag the chain and feel the lash in Cuba for
ever more

And now our money is all gone, we must go to sea
once more
But each man stayed and listened to the voice of
Captain Moore
'There's gold and silver to be had if with me you'll
remain
We'll hoist the pirate flag aloft and scour the Spanish
main.'

We all agreed save five young lads, so they were told
    to land
Two of them were Boston boys and two from
    Newfoundland
The other was an Irish boy belonging to Lismore
I wish that I had joined those lads and gone with
    them ashore

We sank and plundered many a ship upon the
    Spanish main
Caused many a wife and orphan in sorrow to remain
To them we gave no quarter, we gave them watery
    graves
For the saying of our captain was that dead men tell
    no tales

But it's oft I've seen the *Flying Cloud* with the wind
    abaft her beam
With her maintop-gallant and mizzen set, a sight for
    to be seen
The rolling deck beneath my feet, a sailor's joy
    to feel
And the canvas taut in the whistling breeze, logging
    sixteen off the reel

Pursued we were by many a ship, by frigates and
    liners too
Until a British man-of-war, the *Dunmow*, hove in
    view

She fired a shot across our boom as we sailed before
    the wind
Then a chain-shot brought our rigging down and we
    fell far behind

The crew they ranged to quarters as she hove up
    alongside
And soon across our quarter-deck there flowed a
    crimson tide
We fought till Captain Moore was killed and twenty
    of our men
A bombshell set our deck on fire and we had to
    surrender then

And it's now to Newgate we are come, bound down
    with iron chains
For sinking and for plundering of ships on the
    Spanish main
The jury's found us guilty and we are condemned
    to die
Young men, a warning by me take and shun all
    piracy.

IN ITS SHAPE and melody this is a forebitter – a song sung after, not during, work – but in its content it is a gallows ballad. What distinguishes it from the run of gallows ballads is that, in place of a maudlin and clichéd tale, it offers a vivid narrative which has the feel of fact and experience. Doerflinger, in *Shantymen and Shantyboys*, suggested it was based on a chapbook, 'The

Dying Declaration of Nicolas Fernandez', who had sailed under the pirate Benito de Soto.

The ninth verse, describing the speed and grace of the pirate ship under full sail, is a rarity in maritime folk song. But no pirate vessel named the *Flying Cloud* (said in some versions to be a Yankee clipper) and no British man-of-war named the *Dunmow* has been traced.

The tune, which comes from Stan Hugill with a good text, is transposed here from triple to double time. The text has turned up on both sides of the Atlantic. Gavin Greig recovered a somewhat stilted variant in Aberdeenshire, with a tune similar to 'The Banks of Inverurie'. An unusual feature of these versions is the constancy of the narrator's surname, Hollander.

main: ocean. From the sixteenth century to the nineteenth century the area of the western Atlantic containing the major Spanish possessions, with a constant flow of valuable cargoes, was known as the Spanish main

ROUD #1802

THE GOLDEN VANITY

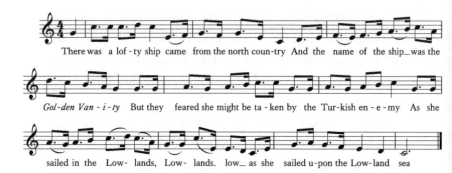

There was a lofty ship came from the north country
And the name of the ship was the *Golden Vanity*
But they feared she might be taken by the Turkish enemy
    As she sailed in the Lowlands, Lowlands low
    As she sailed upon the Lowland sea.

Then up there spoke the little cabin boy
Saying, 'What will you give me if the galley I destroy?'
'O you can wed my daughter who is my pride and joy
    If you sink her in the Lowlands, Lowlands low
    If you sink her in the Lowland sea.'

So the boy bared his breast and he plunged into
    the tide
He swam till he came to the Turkish pirate's side
He climbed on deck and went below, by none was
    he espied
    For to sink her in the Lowlands, Lowlands low
    To sink her in the Lowland sea.

He bored with his auger, he bored once and twice
Some were playing cards and some were at the dice
When the salt water dazzled in their eyes
　　And she sank in the Lowlands, Lowlands low
　　She sank in the Lowland sea.

Then the boy swam back to the starboard side
Saying, 'Captain, take me in, I am drifting with the tide.'
'I will sink you, I will kill you, if you claim my child as bride
　　I will sink you in the Lowlands, Lowlands low
　　I'll sink you in the Lowland sea.'

So the boy swam round to the larboard side
Saying, 'Messmates, take me in, I am drowning in the tide.'
And his messmates took him up, and on the deck he died
　　As they sailed in the Lowlands, Lowlands low
　　As they sailed on the Lowland sea.

ALTHOUGH THE ENEMY ship in this widespread ballad is often identified as Spanish or French, there is no improbability in encountering a Turkish pirate vessel off the coast of northern Europe. By the early seventeenth century, ships from the eastern Mediterranean were repeatedly sailing up the English Channel not only to plunder local shipping but to take men and women from coastal villages for the slave markets, in numbers reckoned at one point to run into thousands.

The oldest known version of the ballad, which is in Samuel Pepys's collection of broadsides, begins:

Sir Walter Rawleigh has built a ship
In the Neatherlands . . .
And it is called the *Sweet Trinity*
And was taken by the gallaly
Sailing in the Neatherlands.

Since pirates were liable to summary justice if there was no court to hand, the cabin boy is free of blame for sinking their ship. But was the captain of the *Golden Vanity* guilty of murdering him? There is no general legal obligation to save someone in danger, however obvious the risk and however easy rescue would be. But here it was the captain who had placed the boy in danger in the first place, and whose motive for withholding rescue was entirely venal. He would not have fared well in the hands of a jury.

This version of the ballad combines a variant collected by Stan Hugill from a shipmate, Jack Birch, and one collected by Alfred Williams from David Sawyer of Ogbourne, Wiltshire, both in the early twentieth century.

The tune was collected by Cecil Sharp in 1908 from Alfred Emery of Othery, Somerset.

CHILD #286   ROUD #122

HENRY MARTIN

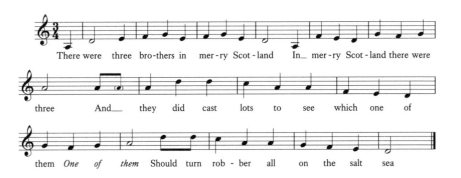

There were three brothers in merry Scotland
In merry Scotland there were three
And they did cast lots to see which one of them
   One of them
Should turn robber all on the salt sea

The lot it fell upon Henry Martin
The youngest of the three
That he should turn robber all on the salt sea
   The salt sea
To maintain his two brothers and he

He hadn't been sailing one cold winter's night
And part of a cold winter's day
Before he espied a tall lofty ship
   Lofty ship
Come bearing on them straight away

'O where are you bound for?' cried Henry Martin
'O where are you bound for?' cried he
'I'm a rich merchant ship and for England I'm bound
    For England I'm bound
If you please will you let me pass by?'

'Now lower your tops'ls, you merchantman bold
And bring yourself under my lee
For I am resolved to plunder you here
    To plunder you here
To maintain my two brothers and me.'

So broadside to broadside to battle they went
They fought for two hours or three
Till at last Henry Martin gave her her death-wound
    Her death-wound
And down to the bottom went she

Sad news, sad news to England is come
Sad news that I bring unto thee
For a lofty tall ship is lost on the salt sea
    The salt sea
And all of her mariners drowned.

A RARITY AMONG ballads, 'Henry Martin' includes no twist of fate – for example Henry finding that his brothers are aboard the merchant ship – and no moral delivered from the scaffold, since he is not even captured. It recounts a simple tragedy: for no good reason a young Scot sets out to plunder shipping;

he encounters and sinks an English merchant ship, sacrificing her entire cargo and crew. Why two of the brothers had to be maintained by the third, and how the third came to command a pirate ship, we are not told in any recovered version. The story is simply one of wasted lives.

In the numerous variants collected in coastal areas of Great Britain (Sharp and Karpeles published a dozen from the West Country alone), two elements recur, albeit not uniformly: the name of Henry Martin (oral tradition is generally casual about names), and the unusual and striking repetition of the final syllables of the third line of each verse.

The present text is an amalgam of a number of collected variants; the tune is the one collected by Sharp in 1906 from Jack Barnard of Bridgwater, Somerset.

CHILD #250   ROUD #104

CAPTAIN WARD AND THE *RAINBOW*

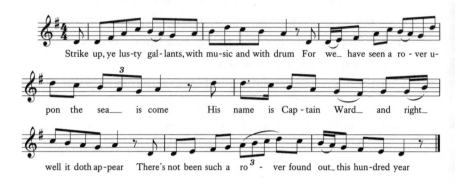

Strike up, ye lus-ty gal-lants, with mu-sic and with drum For we— have seen a ro-ver u-pon the sea— is come His name is Cap-tain Ward— and right— well it doth ap-pear There's not been such a ro - ver found out— this hun-dred year

Strike up, ye lusty gallants, with music and with drum
For we have seen a rover upon the sea is come
His name is Captain Ward and right well it doth
    appear
There's not been such a rover found out this hundred
    year

For he hath sent unto our king the sixth of January
Desiring that he might come in with all his company
'And if the king will let me come until my tale is told
I will bestow as ransom full thirty ton of gold.'

'O nay, o nay,' then said our king 'O nay, this may
    not be
To yield to such a rover I never will agree
He hath deceived the Frenchman, likewise the king
    of Spain
And how should he be true to me that has been false
    to twain.'

And so our king provisioned a ship of worthy fame
The *Rainbow* she is callèd if you would know her name
And now the gallant *Rainbow* she sails upon the sea
Five hundred gallant seamen to be her company

The Dutchman and the Spaniard she made them for
    to flee
Also the bonny Frenchman as she met him on the sea
And when the gallant *Rainbow* did come where Ward
    did lie
'Where is the captain of this ship?' the *Rainbow* she did
    cry

'O that am I,' says Captain Ward, 'There's no man
    bids me lie
And if thou art the king's ship, thou'rt welcome unto me'
'I tell thee what,' says *Rainbow*, 'Our king is in great
    grief
That thou shouldst lie upon the sea and play the
    arrant thief

'You will not let our merchant ships pass as they did
    before
Such tidings to our king has come, which grieves his
    heart full sore.'
With that the gallant *Rainbow* she shot, out of her
    pride,
Full fifty-one brass pieces, all charged on every side

But all these gallant cannon prevailèd not a pin
Though on the outside they were brass, brave Ward
    was steel within
'Shoot on, shoot on,' says Captain Ward, 'Your sport
    well pleaseth me
And he that first gives over shall yield unto the sea

'I never wronged an English ship, but the Turk and
    king of Spain
Also the jovial Dutchman that I met on the main
And if I had known your king a year or two before
I would have saved brave Essex' life, whose death
    did grieve me sore

'Go tell the king of England, go tell him thus
    from me
If he reign king of all the land I will reign king
    at sea.'
With that the gallant *Rainbow* she shot and shot
    in vain
And left the rover's company and returned home
    again

THE HERO OF THIS ballad is not the *Rainbow* (whose captain
is not even named) but the pirate Ward (whose ironclad vessel
is not identified either). Ward's initial offer to turn himself in
with his loot was not a balladeer's invention: in the sixteenth
and seventeenth centuries, a number of pirates were granted
a royal pardon in return for becoming maritime thief-takers.

But the king was probably wise to refuse Ward's offer: more than one such pirate, now furnished with a royal pardon, had gone back to privateering.

John Ward himself was from Kent. He was credited with having in 1604 persuaded the crew of a king's ship in which he was serving to turn to piracy under his command. Little is known of his exploits, but by 1609 he and his fellow pirate Dansekar were being referred to as 'two late famous pirates'. All told, there is not a great deal on which to build a heroic myth. Nor is there known to have been a royal warship in this period named the *Rainbow*. There was, however, a king's ship of that name in the 1620 Algiers expedition. There was also a merchant vessel named the *Rainbow* which was part-owned by the father of the great pirate-hunter and sea-captain of the 1630s, William Rainborough. One of these may perhaps be the ballad's link to history.

The wording given here is, with some trimming, the text of a seventeenth-century blackletter broadside found in the Bagford Ballads, the Pepys collection, the Roxburghe Ballads and elsewhere. Two concluding stanzas about three admirals (Clifford, Mountjoy and Essex) who might have defeated Ward are omitted; they do, however, enable the episode to be located early in the reign of James I and VI.

The ballad has lived in oral tradition and has been collected on both sides of the Atlantic. The melody given here was collected by George Gardiner from Isaac Hobbes of Micheldever, Hants, in 1906.

CHILD #287   ROUD #224

ARSON

Arson is the deliberate firing of a building. Because of the risk that a conflagration would spread, it was a common-law misdemeanour to set fire to your own property. Burning the property of others was a capital felony. Proof of intent, however, was not always easy, given the constant risk of accident in wooden-framed or thatched houses lit by candles or oil lamps and heated by open fires.

While both of the ballads in this section involve deliberate arson, neither tells an obvious or linear story.

In the first, a vendetta is carried by the owners of Frendracht to an extreme that not even the Macbeths contemplated: burning part of their own house down in order to kill their guests. It's in fact one reason why the damning narrative is probably false. But, as ever, the accusation has proved more durable than the simple fact that the fire – which undoubtedly occurred, with its tragic consequences – was probably accidental.

A suitor's resort to arson when his advances are rejected is by no means fanciful, as newspaper readers know. What is unusual about the second ballad is, first, that William (with his sobriquet 'Wise') is a canny enough gambler to anticipate what may happen when he stakes his sister's chastity against Redesdale's land; and, second, that the sister who is almost immolated because of the drunken bet shows courage and coolness in evading its consequences.

THE FIRE OF FRENDRACHT

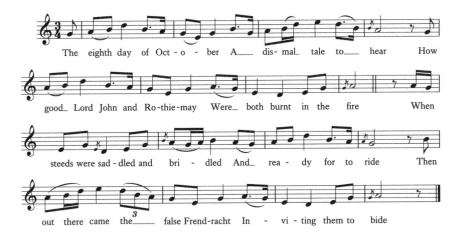

The eighth day of October A— dis- mal— tale to— hear How good— Lord John and Ro-thie-may Were— both burnt in the fire When steeds were sad - dled and bri - dled And— rea - dy for to ride Then out there came the— false Frend-racht In - vi - ting them to bide

The eighth day of October
A dismal tale to hear
How good Lord John and Rothiemay
Were both burnt in the fire

When steeds were saddled and bridled
And ready for to ride
Then out there came the false Frendracht
Inviting them to bide

Saying, 'Stay this night until we sup
The morn until we dine
'Twill be a token of greement
Twixt your good lord and mine.'

When mass was sung and bells were rung
And all men bound for bed
Good Lord John and Rothiemay
In one chamber were laid

They hadna lang cast off their clothes
And were but now asleep
When the dowie reek began to rise
And the joists began to crack

He's ta'en him to the wire-window
And doleful strack and dang
But it would neither bow nor break
The stanchions were so strang

Then out spoke the Lady Frendracht
And loudly she did cry
'The keys are cast in the deep draw-well
Ye canna get away.'

Lady Rothiemay came on the morn
She kneeled upon the green
'Restore your lodgers, false Frendracht
That ye burned yestereen

'O were I like yon turtle dove
And had I wings to fly
I'd fly about the false Frendracht
Crying vengeance till I die

'Frendracht false, all through the ha's
I wish you'd sink for sin
For first you killed my own good lord
And now you've burned my son

'I caredna muckle for my lord
I saw him laid in clay
But a' is for my own dear son
The heir o' Rothiemay.'

THERE WAS A LONG-RUNNING vendetta between the Crichtons of Frendracht and the Gordons of Rothiemay, whose lands lay on opposite sides of the river Deveron, the boundary between Aberdeenshire and Banffshire. A dispute during the 1620s over fishing rights spilled over into bloodshed but was settled by the mediation of the Marquis of Huntly. It included a blood-money payment by the Crichtons to the Gordons, but a dispute then arose about its distribution. Huntly tried without success to mediate again, and then sent his own son and the Gordons' son to protect the Crichtons on their return to Frendracht. Arrived there, the two young men were pressed by the Crichtons to stay the night; but during the night (8–9 October 1630), the tower where the guests were sleeping caught fire and they and their servants were burned to death.

The ballad propagates the widespread belief that it was the Crichtons who had set fire to their own dwelling in order to kill the heir to Rothiemay.

The text, variously recorded by Motherwell, Maidment and Kinloch, has called for a fair amount of amalgamation and condensation, but the drama and some of the poetry merit it. The tune is the first strain of the melody printed by Christie from Banffshire tradition.

CHILD #196

REDESDALE AND WISE WILLIAM

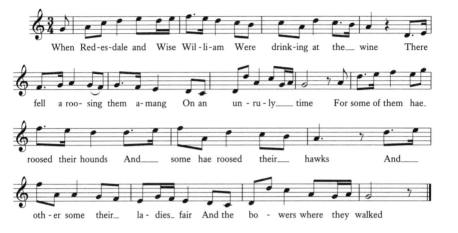

When Red-es-dale and Wise Wil-li-am Were drink-ing at the__ wine There fell a roo- sing them a-mang On an un - ru - ly__ time For some of them hae__ roosed their hounds And__ some hae roosed their__ hawks And__ oth - er some their__ la - dies__ fair And the bo - wers where they walked

When Redesdale and Wise William
Were drinking at the wine
There fell a roosing them amang
On an unruly time
For some of them hae roosed their hounds
And some hae roosed their hawks
And other some their ladies fair
And the bowers where they walked

Then it's out and spak him Redesdale
'I'll wad my lands wi' thee
I'll wad my lands against thy head
And this is what I'll dee
There is no lady in the land
In bower where'er she be
That I could not her favour win
Wi' ae blink o' my e'e.'

Says William 'I've an ae sister
She's fair, baith e'e and bree
And ye'll no wed her wi'out courting
Wi' ae blink o' your e'e.'

Then Redesdale took Wise William
Bound him in prison strang
That he might neither gang nor ride
Nor ae word to her send
But he has written a braid letter
Between the night and day
And sent it to his own sister
By dun feather and gray

The firsten line she looked on
A licht lauchter ga'e she
But e'er she read it tae the end
The tear blinded her e'e
'Come to me, my maidens all
Come hitherward to me
For here it comes him Redesdale
Who comes a-courting me.'

'Come down, come down, my lady fair
Ae sicht o' you to see
And bonny are the gowns o' silk
That I will give to thee.'
'If you have bonny gowns o' silk
Then mine are bonny tee
Gae from my yetts now, Redesdale
For me you shall not see.'

'Come down, come down, my lady fair
A sight o' you I'll see
And bonny are the lands sae broad
That I will give to thee.'
'If you have bonny lands sae broad
Then mine are bonny tee
Go from my yetts now Redesdale
For me ye shall not see.'

'Come down, come down, ye lady fair
A sicht o' you to see
Or I will set your bower on fire
Atween your nurse and thee.'
And he has set her bower on fire
And quickly did it flame
He's turned his horse's head about
Saying they'll no get out again

'Come hitherwards, my maidens fair
Come hither unto me
For through this reek and through this smeek
It's through it we must be.'
They took wet mantles them about
Their coffers by the band
And through the reek and through the flame
Alive they all have won

When they had got out through the fire
And able all to stand
She sent a maid to Wise William
To bruik Lord Redesdale's land

'Your land is mine now, Redesdale
For I have won them free
If there's a good woman in the world
My ae sister is she.'

ALTHOUGH THE TEXT of this ballad was published by Buchan in 1828 as given to him from memory by a Strichen informant named Nicol, and was also found by Child in full form in the Harris manuscript and in fragmentary form in Kinloch's, no melody was ever recorded or noted for it. Its opening stanzas, however, are almost replicated in 'Young Allan' (Child #245), for which Christie gives the tune we have used here, 'from the singing of an old woman of Buckie, Banffshire, who died at 80 in 1866; her father was a famous ballad-singer in Buckie in the eighteenth century.'

The present lyric is a compound of the Buchan and Harris texts, neither of which is free of imperfections. In particular, neither comes to a well-made end. The collation also omits, for purely practical reasons, a series of elegant verses, which can be found in Child, in which multiple gifts are offered and rejected in classic ballad form.

roosing: bragging, wagering
wad: pledge
ae: only
braid letter: a letter on a broadsheet
yetts: gates

e'e and bree: eye and brow
tee: too
smeek: smoke
bruik: possess, enjoy
won: arrived

CHILD #246

FALSE ACCUSATION

U ntil the setting-up during the nineteenth century of local constabularies paid out of public funds, the chief source of prosecution evidence was informers who, as the saying was, would swear a life away for money. The payment was usually offered by one of the numerous prosecution societies, with the aid of which more prosperous citizens (including many magistrates) sought to keep down local crime.

The accused, for their part, had little protection. John Lilburne in the years of the Long Parliament had fought with success to let the accused see the indictment; but by the time of the Napoleonic Wars the courts had stultified the right by charging exorbitant sums for copies in advance of trial. While barristers were commonly briefed by prosecutors, on felony charges (which included most thefts) other than treason there was historically no right to counsel for the accused: hence the absence of defence lawyers from the gallows and trial ballads. The accused themselves were not entitled (until 1898, in fact) to give sworn evidence in their own defence: all they could do was question the informer from the dock. There was no presumption of innocence and no requirement of proof beyond reasonable doubt. A capital trial rarely took more than an hour or two.

Informing, both by local individuals and by professional thief-takers, and not only privately but from the witness box, thus became a profitable racket, at least until, towards the end of the eighteenth century, advocates like William Garrow began to force their way into the criminal process, and the concept of a fundamental right to be defended, and to have a case properly proved by credible testimony, began to take root. Although lawyers, perhaps deservedly, do not get a good press, it was their over-representation in Parliament and their social proximity to the judges which made this possible. Under the ever-present shadow of the gallows, the transports and the prison hulks, they were able by the 1830s to establish as fundamental rights the entitlement of accused persons to a defence, to a presumption of innocence, and to independent proof of guilt beyond reasonable doubt.

HUGH THE GRAEME

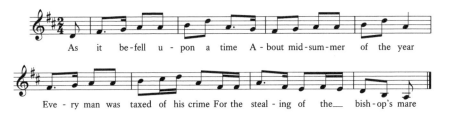

As it befell upon a time About mid-sum-mer of the year

Eve - ry man was taxed of his crime For the steal - ing of the— bish-op's mare

As it befell upon a time
About midsummer of the year
Every man was taxed of his crime
For the stealing of the bishop's mare

Good Lord Scroope's to the hunting gane
Over the moors and mountains clear
And he has grippit Hugh the Graeme
For stealing of the bishop's mare

They hae tied him hand and foot
And led him into Carlisle town
The lads and lasses stood on the walls
Crying 'Hugh the Graeme thou'll ne'er go down.'

But they hae chosen a jury of men
'Mongst all their best nobility
The twelve of them cried out at once
'Sir Hugh the Graeme he now must die.'

Then it's up and spak the Lady Hume
As she sat by the bishop's knee

'Five hundred measures of gold I'll give
To grant Sir Hugh the Graeme to me.'

'O hold your tongue' the bishop says
'And ye'll let a' your pleadings be
Though a' the Graemes were in this court
He should be hangit high for me.'

They've ta'en him to the gallows-knoll
He's lookit to the gallows tree
Yet never colour left his cheek
Nor ever did he blink his e'e

He's lookit owre his left shoulder
It was to see what he might see
And there he saw his old father
And he was weeping bitterly

'O hold your tongue, my old father
And with your weeping let it be
Thy weeping's sairer on my heart
Than a' that they can do to me

'Remember me to Maggie my wife
The next time ye gang o'er the moor
She is the cause I lose my life
She with the bishop played the whore

'Ye'll give my brother John the sword
That's pointed with the metal clear

And bid him come at eight of the clock
To see me pay the bishop's mare

And Johnnie Armstrong tak' my sword
That's pointed with the metal fine
And when ye come to the English side
Remember the death of Hugh the Graeme.'

THE GRAEMES (or Grahams) were Scottish borderers with a reputation as cattle-rustlers and horse-thieves. The poet Allan Cunningham thought this was quite enough to explain why Hugh was tried and hanged; the back-story, he said, was 'unnecessary and superfluous'.

William Stenhouse, in his notes to Johnson's *Scots Musical Museum*, did not agree. 'According to tradition,' he wrote,

Robert Aldridge, Bishop of Carlisle about the year 1560 [in fact he died in 1555], seduced the wife of Hugh Graham . . . Graham, being unable to bring so powerful a prelate to justice, in revenge made an excursion into Cumberland and carried off, inter alia, a fine mare belonging to the bishop; but being closely pursued by Sir John Scroope, warden of Carlisle, with a party on horseback, was apprehended near Solway Moss, and carried to Carlisle, where he was tried and convicted of felony. Great intercessions were made to save his life, but the bishop, it is said, being determined to remove the chief obstacle to his guilty passions, remained inexorable, and poor Graham fell a victim to his own indiscretion and his wife's infidelity.

Child suspected that Stenhouse's account was simply taken from the ballad, with the bishop's name added for verisimilitude. He was influenced by the fact that the ballad is not found in print until the mid-seventeenth century, but this is true of a good many older ballads. There is nothing historically implausible in Hugh being accused, truly or falsely, of stealing the bishop's mare and being brought to summary trial before a hand-picked jury and a bench on which the bishop himself sat. Two centuries later, Lord Mansfield presided over the trial of the alleged rioters who had burned down his house.

The text here is collated from Child's variants. In *Pills to Purge Melancholy* (1706) the tune is given as 'Chevy Chase', but the one used here is the first (and probably more authentic) strain of the Banffshire melody given in Christie's *Traditional Ballad Airs*.

grippit: seized

CHILD #191   ROUD #84

THE SHEFFIELD APPRENTICE

I was brought up at Sheffield but not of high degree
My parents doted on me, they had no child but me
I rode about for pleasure and where my fancy led
Till I was bound apprentice, then all my joys were fled

I did not like my master, he did not use me well
I made a resolution not long with him to dwell
And unknown to my parents, from him I ran away
I steered my course to London, and cursed be the day

When I came into London a lady met me there
She offered me great wages to serve her for a year
Deluded by her promises, with her I did agree
To go with her to Holland, which proved my destiny

We had not left old England a year but two or three
Before my wealthy mistress grew very fond of me

She said her gold and silver, her houses and her land
If I'd consent to have her, should be at my command

I said 'My honoured lady, I cannot wed you both
For I'm already promised and have made a solemn oath
To wed with none but Sally, your handsome
      chambermaid
Believe me now, dear mistress, she has my heart
      betrayed.'

My mistress in a passion away from me did go
She swore she'd be revenged on me and work my
      overthrow
So much perplexed in humour she could not be my wife
She swore she'd find a project to take away my life

As I walked in the garden just at the dawn of day
My mistress stood a-watching the pretty flowers gay
A gold ring from her finger, as I was passing by
She slipped it in my pocket, and for it I must die

My mistress swore I'd robbed her and straightway
      I was brought
Before a grave old justice to answer for my fault
Long time I pleaded guiltless but I could not prevail
My mistress swore against me and I was sent to gaol

Before the last assizes 'tis tried I was and cast
And then the heavy sentence of death on me was
      passed

From thence for execution they have dragged me to
    the tree
May God reward my mistress, for she has ruined me

All you that stand around me my cruel fate to see
Don't glory in my downfall but rather pity me
Believe me, I am innocent, I bid this world adieu
Farewell my dearest Sally, I die for love of you.

AS LONG AGO AS 1656 Oliver Cromwell told Parliament:
'There are wicked and abominable laws that will be in your
power to alter. To hang a man for sixpence, thirteen pence, I
know not what . . . This is a thing God will reckon for.' Theft
of goods worth more than twelve pence (that is, a shilling)
constituted the felony of grand larceny and so for centuries
meant hanging. In spite of eventual limitations on the use of
the death penalty, the arbitrary cruelty of the law persisted
until the distinction between grand and petty larceny was
abolished in 1861.

The text used here, with some patching from the version
given to Gavin Greig by Bell Robertson of New Pitsligo, is from
an eighteenth-century broadside in the Madden collection.
The tune comes, via Ewan MacColl, from his father, William
Miller of Stirling.

ROUD #399

THE BLACK VELVET BAND

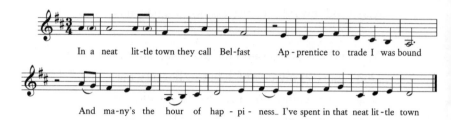

In a neat little town they call Belfast
Apprentice to trade I was bound
And many's the hour of happiness
I've spent in that neat little town

A sad misfortune came over me
And caused me stray from the land
Far away from my friends and relations
Betrayed by a black velvet band

I took a stroll down the Broadway
Meaning not long for to stay
When who should I see but a pretty
    young maid
Come tripping along the highway

She was both fair and handsome
Her neck it was like to a swan
And her hair hung over her shoulder
Held up by a black velvet band

I took a stroll with this fair pretty maid
A gentleman passing us by
I could see she meant to do for him
By the look in her roguish black eye

His watch she took from his pocket
And placed it right into my hand
And the very next words that I spoke were
'Bad luck to the black velvet band.'

Before the judge and jury
Next morning I had to appear
The judge he said to me 'Young man
Your case it is proven clear

You'll have seven years penal servitude
To be spent far away from this land
Far away from your friends and relations
Transported to Van Diemen's Land

So come all you dashing young fellows
I'd have you take warning by me
When you are out on the liquor, my boys
Beware of them pretty colleens

They'll treat you to strong drink, my boys
Till you are not able to stand
And before you know it they'll have you
Transported to Van Diemen's Land.'

A. L. LLOYD surmised that this ballad originated as a late Victorian stage song – a view supported more by the waltz-time melody than by the broadside-like lyric. Certainly it's a long time since anyone could call Belfast 'a neat little town'.

It is possible that the narrator has simply been caught with a stolen watch, but much more probable that the girl with the black velvet band was working with the owner of the watch, the two of them sharing the reward money for securing a conviction.

The present version is based on that of the Norfolk singer Harry Cox.

ROUD #2146

INCEST

I ncest was from an early date an ecclesiastical offence, pun-
ishable by excommunication; but, apart from a shortlived
criminalization under the Commonwealth in 1650, it was not
made a crime in England and Wales until 1908. It features
rarely in British folk song. When it does, it is between brother
and sister, not (as it is now believed chiefly to occur) between
generations; and it is always the sister who pays the ultimate
price.

Francis James Child recorded six incest ballads: 'Babylon'
(#14), 'Sheath and Knife' (#16), 'Lizzie Wan' (#51), 'The
King's Dochter Lady Jean' (#52), 'The Bonny Hind' (#50)
and 'Brown Robyn's Confession' (#57). These have been the
subject of an illuminating study by Professor Ruth Perry in
Eighteenth Century: Theory and Interpretation (XLVII/2–3).
Taking the extant texts in broad chronological sequence, she
notes 'a marked change in the quality of brother-sister rela-
tionships in the course of 150 years, resulting in a diminution
of the sister's agency in the latter period as well as a starker,
more tragic outcome to their story of illicit incest'. There is
also a divide between the 'accidental incest' narratives, where

the victim of a rape turns out to be a sibling (for example 'Babylon'), and the 'true love' brother-and-sister narratives, of which 'Sheath and Knife' and 'Lizzie Wan' are the present examples, though here too the brother's readiness to shift guilt to the sister is striking.

SHEATH AND KNIFE

A

There was a sister and a brother
The sun goes to under the wood
Who most entirely lovèd other
God give we never had been sib

He says, 'Sister, I would lay thee by
The sun goes to under the wood
And thou would not my deeds cry.'
God give we never had been sib

'Alas brother would ye do so
The sun goes to under the wood
I had rather death now undergo
Alas if we had never been sib

'The morn it is my father's feast
The sun goes to under the hill
While in my clothes I must be least
God give we never had been sib

'When they convening all at once
To royal feasting in the hall
It me behoveth them amongst
Go deckèd in a gown of pall

'And when I lout me to my toe
The sun goes to under the hill
My lesse will brak and go in two
God give we never had been sib

'And when I lout me to my knee
The sun goes to under the hill
My lace will brak and go in three
God give we never had been sib

'And it will go from one till other
The sun goes to under the hill
Until it come to John my brother
Lord give we never had been sib

'And John my brother is most ill
The sun goes to under the hill
He will us both burn on a hill
God give we never had been sib

'I shall go to my father's stable
The sun goes to under the hill
And take a steed both wight and able
Lord give we never had been sib

'And we shall ride till time we spend
The sun goes to under the hill
Until we see our trystis end.'
God give we never had been sib

She had not ridden a mile but ane
The sun goes to under the hill
When she gan quaking, groan and groan
God give we never had been sib

'Is there water in your shoes
The sun goes to under the hill
Or comes the wind into your gloves
God give we never had been sib

'Or think you me too simple a knight
The sun goes to under the hill
To ride or go with you all night?'
God give we never had been sib

'And when ye hear me loud loud cry
The sun goes to under the hill
Ye'll bend your bow and run thereby
God give we never had been sib

And when ye see me lie full still
The sun goes to under the hill
So sound your horn and come me till.'
God give we never had been sib

'I would give all my father's land
The sun goes to under the hill
For one woman at my command.'
God give we never had been sib

When that he cam soon her beside
The sun goes down under the wood
The babe was born, the lady dead
God give we never had been sib

Then he has ta'en his young young son
The sun goes down under the wood
And borne him to a milk woman
God give we never had been sib

He drew his sword, him wounding sore
The sun goes down under the wood
From this time to ride never more
God give we never had been sib

'Mother, quoth he, canst thou mak my bed
The sun goes down under the wood
So make it long and nothing broad.
God give we never had been sib

'Mother alas I tint my knife
The sun goes down under the wood
I lovèd better than my life
God give we never had been sib

'Mother alas I have tint my sheath
The sun goes down under the wood
I lovèd better than them baith.
God give we never had been sib

There is no cutler in this land
The sun goes down under the hill
Can make a knife so at my command
God give we never had been sib

He turned and facèd to the wa'
The sun goes down under the hill
Gave up the ghost and gaed his way.
God give we never had been sib

The one was laid in Mary kirk
The other in Mary choir
Out through the one there grew a birk
And out through the other a briar.

* * *

sib: in Middle English, any close relationship, including, as here, siblings
lout: bend, bow

wight: strong
lesse: lace
tint: lost

B

It is whispered in parlour, it's whispered in ha'
The broom blooms bonny, the broom blooms fair
That the king's dochter gaes wi' child to her brither
And we darena gae down tae the broom ony mair

He's ta'en his sister tae her father's deer park
The broom blooms bonny, the broom blooms fair
Wi' his yew-tree bow fast slung to his back
And we darena gae down tae the broom ony mair

Now it's when ye hear me gie a loud cry
The broom blooms bonny, the broom blooms fair
Then bend your bow and let your arrow fly
And we darena gae down to the broom ony mair

And when that ye see me lying still
The broom blooms bonny, the broom blooms fair
Then ye may come and greet your fill
And we darena gae down to the broom ony mair

He has made a grave that was long and was deep
The broom blooms bonny, the broom blooms fair
And buried his sister with her babe at her feet
And we darena gae down to the broom ony mair

And when he came to his father's hall
The broom blooms bonny, the broom blooms fair
There was music and minstrels and dancing and all
And we darena gae down to the broom ony mair

'O Willie, o Willie what makes thee in pain?'
The broom blooms bonny, the broom blooms fair
'I have lost sheath and knife that I'll ne'er see again.'
And we darena gae down to the broom ony mair

'There is ships o' your father's sailing on the sea
The broom blooms bonny, the broom blooms fair
That will bring as good sheath and a knife unto thee.'
And we darena gae down to the broom ony mair

'There is ship's o' my father's sailing on the sea
The broom blooms bonny, the broom blooms fair
But sic sheath and knife they can never bring to me.'
And we darena gae down to the broom ony mair

greet: weep

VARIANT A, the oldest known version of this ballad, is the manuscript text reproduced by Ruth Perry (see the introductory note) from Robert Edwards's commonplace book, circa 1630, except for some orthographic and textual changes needed for clarity. It contains distinct elements of the ballad of 'Leesome Brand' (Child #15), which again revolves around an illicit pregnancy; but in 'Sheath and Knife' the child survives and is given to a wet-nurse.

Ruth Perry has noted that the first refrain line reproduces a thirteenth-century lyric: 'Nou goth sonne under wode'.

VARIANT B comes principally from the version taken down by Motherwell in 1821 from Mrs King of Kilbarchan, supplemented by the version recalled by Walter Scott (with the reservation that Scott left little traditional material unchanged) and noted in Sharpe's *Ballad Book*.

The Edwards manuscript, from which variant A comes, gives no tune. The only known melody is the one supplied by Robert Burns and reproduced as 'The Broom Blooms Bonie' (#461) in James Johnson's *Scots Musical Museum*. It makes an acceptable fit with variant **B**, to which we have set it here, but not with variant **A**: hence our setting of variant **A** to Kinloch's tune (1827) for 'Babylon' (Child #14), sourced by Kinloch simply as 'sung in Mearnsshire'.

CHILD #16   ROUD #3960

LIZZIE WAN

Liz-zie Wan___ sits at her fa-ther's bow-er door___ Wee-ping and mak- ing___ mane   And   by there cam   her   fa-ther dear   'What ails thee Liz-zie   Wan?'

Lizzie Wan sits at her father's bower door
Weeping and making mane
And by there cam her father dear
'What ails thee Lizzie Wan?'

'I ail, I ail, dear father,' she said
'And I'll tell you the reason why
There is a child between my sides
Between my dear Billy and I.'

Now Lizzie sits at her father's bower door
Sighing and making mane
And by there cam her brother dear
'What ails thee Lizzie Wan?'

'I ail, I ail, dear brither,' she said
'And I'll tell you the reason why
There is a child between my sides
Between you, dear Billy, and I.'

'And hast thou told father and mother of that?
And hast thou told sae of me?'

And he has drawn his gude braid sword
That hang down by his knee

And he has cut of Lizzie Wan's head
And her fair body in three
And he's awa' to his mother's bower
And sair aghast was he.

'What ails thee, what ails thee, Billy Wan
What ails thee sae fast to run?
For I see by thy ill colour
Some felon's deed thou hast done.'

'Some felon's deed have I done, mother,
And I pray you pardon me
For I've cut off my greyhound's head
Since he wadna rin by me.'

'Thy greyhound's bluid was ne'er sae red
O my son Billy Wan
For I see by thy ill colour
Some felon's deed thou hast done.'

'Some felon's deed have I done, mother,
And I pray you pardon me
For I hae cut off Lizzie Wan's head
And her fair body in three.'

'O what wilt thou do when your father comes hame
O my son Billy Wan?'

'I'll set my foot in a bottomless boat
And swim to the sea-ground.'

'And when will thou come hame again
O my son Billy Wan?
The sun and moon shall dance on the green
The night that I come hame.'

THIS TEXT OF A BALLAD rare in oral tradition was taken by Child from Herd's MS and *Scottish Songs* (1776). The resolution of the story echoes the 'Lord Randal' group of ballads.

The tune given here was collected by Cecil Sharp and Maud Karpeles from Benjamin Finlay in Kentucky in 1917.

'Felon's deed' is substituted here for Herd's 'fallow's deed', a phrase which Child could not recognize and was probably wrongly transcribed.

CHILD #51   ROUD #234

THE KING'S DOCHTER LADY JEAN

La - dy— Jean sits in her— bow-er win-dow Se - wing her silk - en—
seam She's look - it out of her bow - er— win-dow And she
saw the leaves grow green *My love* *And she saw* *the lea-ves* *grow* *green*

Lady Jean she sits in her bower window
Sewing her silken seam
She's lookit out of her bower window
And she saw the leaves grow green
> *My love*
> *And she saw the leaves grow green*

She's stuck the needle in her sleeve
The seam down by her toe
And she's awa' to the merry greenwood
To pull the nut and sloe

She hadna pu'd a nut at a'
A nut but scarcely three
When out and spak a braw young man
And a braw young man was he

'How dare ye shake the leaves,' he said,
'How dare ye brak the tree

How dare ye pluck the nuts,' he said
'Without the leave of me.'

It's 'I will pull the nut,' she said
'And I will bow the tree
And I will come to the merry greenwood
And ask nae leave of thee.'

He gript her by the middle sae sma'
And by the grass-green sleeve
And laid her low in the good greenwood
And of her asked nae leave

She says, 'Young man, what is your name
For ye've brought me meikle shame
For I am the king's youngest dochter
And this nicht I daurna gang hame.'

'If ye be the king's young dochter,' he said,
'I am his auldest son
And heavy, heavy is the deed
That you and I have done.

The first time I cam hame, Jeanie
Thou wasna here nor born
I wish my pretty ship had sunk
And I had been forlorn.'

He had a penknife in his hand
Hang low down by his gair

And between the long rib and the short
He woundit her deep and sair.

THIS VERSION combines two variants collected by Motherwell, both of them imperfect. In one (used here) the brother reacts to the revelation by stabbing his sister. In the other, the sister stabs herself:

She put her hand down by her side
And down into her spare
And she's pu'd out a wee pen-knife
And wounded herself full sair

The tune is printed in Motherwell's appendix (1827), as taken down by Andrew Blaikie of Paisley.

forlorn: lost
spare: opening in a garment
gair: clothing

CHILD #52   ROUD #39

CHEATS AND THIEVES

From an early date the judge-made common law criminalized fraud – deceiving someone into parting with money or goods or land. But it also had a special category for cheats. 'Cheat' referred not to the perpetrator but to the methodical use of false measures or weights, which affected the public at large.

For centuries, market crimes were vigorously prosecuted. They included not only cheats but regrating, engrossing and forestalling (buying up all the corn, butter and so on at a market, or on its way to market, in order to resell it at an inflated price). The judges recognized the potential for civil disorder if these activities were tolerated. But from the end of the eighteenth century, first politicians and eventually judges started to accept that the criminal law could not stand in the way of free markets, and market crimes became obsolete.

The three rogues in the first song in this section were classic swindlers in trades peculiarly open to such practices – milling, weaving and tailoring. But a broadside printed by Kendrew in York circa 1830 lists numerous other trades whose practitioners could not be trusted: lawyers, doctors, pawnbrokers, grocers, butchers, bakers, barbers, hucksters and even wheelwrights.

The Lochmaben harper who cheated the king of his best horse was a case apart. For the rest, sailors ashore were prime targets, with time enough when next at sea to rue their experience in song.

THE THREE JOLLY ROGUES

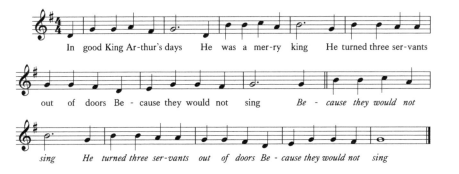

In good King Arthur's days
He was a merry king
He turned three servants out of doors
Because they would not sing

Because they would not sing
He turned three servants out of doors
Because they would not sing

The first one was a miller
The second was a weaver
And the third one was a little tailòr
Three thieving rogues together

The miller he stole meal
And the weaver he stole yarn
And the little tailòr he stole broadcloth
To keep them three rogues warm

Well the miller drowned in his dam
And the weaver hanged in his yarn
But the Devil put his hand on the little tailòr
With the broadcloth under his arm

Now the miller still floats in his dam
And the weaver still hangs in his yarn
But the little tailòr he skips through hell
With a broadcloth under his arm

ALTHOUGH THIS SONG has the air of a nursery song – and may well have had such origins (see the notes to #113 in the *New Penguin Book of English Folk Songs*) – it is about something of real concern to ordinary folk: the filching of corn or meal by millers to whom it was entrusted for grinding; of yarn by weavers who were hired to make cloth of it; and of cloth by tailors who were hired to make clothes of it. The latter were reckoned to get away with cheating so often that the Devil must be their protector.

The text and tune are from oral tradition.

ROUD #130

MAGGIE MAY

I was paid off at the pool in the port of Liverpool
Three pounds ten and sixpence was my pay
When I saw the tin I grinned
But I very soon got skinned
By a girl by the name of Maggie May

Oh Maggie Maggie May
They've taken you away
They've sent you to Van Diemen's cruel shore
For you've robbed so many a sailor
And skinned so many a whaler
Now you'll never shine in Paradise Street no more

The first time I saw Maggie she took my breath away
She was cruising up and down Canning Place
With a figure as divine
As a frigate of the line
So being a sailor I gave chase

In the morning I awoke, I was flat and stony broke
No jacket, trousers, waistcoat could I find
When I asked her where they were
She answered 'My dear sir
They're down in Kelly's knocker, number nine.'

Oh Maggie Maggie May
They've taken you away
They've sent you to Van Diemen's cruel shore
For the jury guilty found her
Of robbing a homeward-bounder
And she'll never shine in Paradise Street no more

THE MANY VERSIONS of 'Maggie May' all derive more or less directly from the abolitionist song 'Nellie Gray', composed in 1856 by the American Benjamin Hanby while he was a student in Ohio. The melody gained a new lease of life in England towards 1870 when it was used for Joe Wilson's song 'Keep Yer Feet Still, Geordie Hinny'. But while Nellie Gray is a Kentucky slave who has been sold down the river and is mourned in lavishly sentimental tones by her lover, Maggie May is a sexy predator whose victims are invariably drunk and rueful sailors.

Nevertheless, a competent lawyer should have been able to get Maggie acquitted of theft: she has no intention of depriving the sailor of his clothing – she tells him exactly where he can find it – and she has a reasonable claim on the pawn money for overnight lodging. She is certainly not guilty of robbery, which requires the use or threat of force. If the only evidence against her was what we find in the song, the judge should have stopped the case.

In *Shanties from the Seven Seas* Stan Hugill gives a wealth of detail about the variant texts, which locate Maggie's activities in a variety of ports. Hugill notes that her name was sometimes Nellie Ray, an echo of the abolitionist lyric. He also notes evidence that 'Maggie May' might actually have antedated Hanby's 'Nellie Gray', for Northcote Parkinson in *The Trade Winds* recorded having seen the lyric in the diary of an able seaman aboard a convict ship bound in 1830 for Van Diemen's Land – and transportation to Australia had ended three years before Hanby published 'Nellie Gray'.

knocker: pawnshop

ROUD #1757

TOM'S GONE TO HILO

Oh Tommy's gone on a whaling ship
Away down Hilo

Oh Tommy's gone on a damn long trip
Tom's gone to Hilo

He never kissed his girl goodbye
He left her and he told her why

She'd robbed him blind and left him broke
He'd had enough, gave her the poke

She drank and boozed his pay away
With a weather-eye on his next payday

His half-pay went, it went like chaff
She hung around for the other half

He shipped away around Cape Horn
His boots and clothes was all in pawn

This tart will get another flame
And she will treat him just the same

Oh Tommy's gone and he's left her flat
Oh Tommy's gone and he'll not be back.

THIS version of an old tale was given to Stan Hugill by Bill Dowling of Bootle. Hilo (pronounced 'Hee-lo') is a coastal town on Hawaii.

The song, a topsail halyard shanty, 'never found favour with the afterguard', according to Hugill, 'as it took too long to hoist a yard to it on account of the slow and lethargic way in which it was sung by a good shantyman. It was rather difficult to sing correctly, but even so it was popular with the crowd, particularly for heavy lifts.'

In spite of Tom's sorry state, and notwithstanding the harsh fate of port prostitutes like Maggie May, his girl may well have committed no crime: 'robbed him blind' was the sailors' way of blaming good-time women for their own profligacy with a pocketful of pay after months at sea.

The song was sentimentalized in later years as a concert piece:

Tommy's gone, what shall I do?
Tommy's gone and I'll go too.

ROUD #481

THE LOCHMABEN HARPER

There was a harper, there was a blind harper He lived in Loch-ma-ben town__ A
wa - ger he laid with lord and laird He'd steal King Hen - ry's wan - ton brown
There he sat in the pub on an eve - ning He_was drunk and drin - king wine__
Lay - ing a wa - ger with these two__ men Straight -way he'd steal the wan - ton brown

There was a harper, there was a blind harper
He lived in Lochmaben town
A wager he laid with lord and laird
He'd steal King Henry's wanton brown

There he sat in the pub on an evening
He was drunk and drinking wine
Laying a wager with these two men
Straightway he'd steal the wanton brown

One of them bet him house and land
And the other one bet five thousand pound
And how they laughed as the silly blind harper
Ran off to steal the wanton brown

Up and spoke the harper's wife
And what a wily one was she

'Take you the mare that's newly foaled
And leave her babe at home with me.'

So he took his harp all in his hand
And he ran playing all round the town
And the king in his high window
His ears were touched by all that sound

'Come in, come in now, you John Harper
More of your music we would hear.'
'Yes that I will,' says John Harper
'But I must have stabling for my mare.'

'You go down to the outer court
That stands a bit below the town
You can leave her warm and snug
Next to my own wanton brown.'

So he's gone down to the outer court
That stands a bit below the town
And there he spied the stable snug
Where stately stood the wanton brown

And he's ta'en out a good strong halter
How the horse come to his call
As he slipped it o'er the wanton's nose
And tied the end to his mare's tail

So there he played in the king's high hall
And he has played them deep asleep

He's gone down on hands and knees
And he's crawled out into the street

He's gone down to the outer court
That stands a bit below the town
And the guards slept as he led out the mare
Tied safe to the wanton brown

Says, 'You'll run through moss, you'll run
    through mire
Through many's the bog and lairy hole
And don't you let this wanton slack
Till you get home to your own foal.'

Soon as the door he has unshut
The mare ran prancing through the town
And there behind, keeping close
She towed the stately wanton brown

They ran through moss, they ran through
    mire
Through many's the bog and lairy hole
She never let the wanton slack
Till she got home to her own foal

John slept in the king's high hall
Till the king called him and aloud
    did cry
'Awake, awake now, John Harper
  For we have slept till nearly day

'Get up, get up now, John Harper
More of your music we would hear.'
'Yes, that I will,' says John Harper
But I must go see to my grey mare.'

So he's gone down to the outer court
And back he's come with many's the tear
'Thieves broke into the outer court
And stole away my good grey mare.'

'O my soul,' then cries the king
If there be thieves all in this town
And if they've taken your grey mare
Then they'll have stole my wanton brown

'Play, play now, you John Harper
Give me music to my ear
I will pay you for your song
And three times more for your grey mare.'

So John played and John got paid
And John ran harping from the town
And never did King Henry think
He'd stolen away his wanton brown

The lords looked o'er the high town wall
They beheld both dale and down
And there they spied this John Harper
Walking back down through the town

'O my soul,' then cries the lord
'How come you come home so very soon?
We see you have no good grey mare
And still you have no wanton brown'

'You lie you lie,' then cries the boy
'For I took him so suddenly
I was paid for my music
Three times for my grey mare.'

He's ta'en them to his own stable
Open wide the door he flung
And there's the mare and there's the foal
And there's the stately wanton brown

One of them paid up house and land
The other one paid five thousand pound
And how he laughed did John Harper
Who stole away the wanton brown.

LOCHMABEN is a small town near Lockerbie in Dumfries and Galloway. The song is a literal border ballad, for in almost all its many recovered versions the harper crosses from Lochmaben into England to steal King Henry's prized horse, the 'wanton brown', and fetch it back to his own stable. He does it by the simple ruse of tethering the horse to his mare, whom he has parted from her foal and who, once liberated, will do anything to get home to it.

'Blind Harpers,' Martin Carthy notes, 'were people who touted for money on the streets as blind people. Some were actually blind and some made music (not all). They were buskers.'

This is Martin's version of the ballad, set by him to a bagpipe tune, 'Follow My Highland Soldier', which he found in a tune-book in Edinburgh. He notes, 'I usually sing the first part of the tune twice and the second part once, and it seems to work well.'

wanton: spirited　**lairy:** mired, boggy

CHILD #192　ROUD #85

THE OYSTER GIRL

As I was a-walking in yonder street so high
A pretty young girlie she chancèd to pass by
A creelie on her back, an Englishman she spied
And she cried 'Will ye buy my oysters?'

'Oysters?' said he, 'Aye, oysters,' said she
'How many oysters for one ha'penny?'
'To some I give one, to others two or three
According to the size of my oysters.'

'Oh,' said the Englishman, 'Well,' said he
'If you will come down to yon tavern with me
It's there we will sit and merry merry be
With white bread and wine to our oysters.'

'O yes,' said the oyster girl, 'O yes,' said she
'It's I will come down to yon tavern with thee
I'll come to the tavern where merry we will be
And get white bread and wine to our oysters.'

He called for the drawboy 'O drawboy,' said he
'Have you got a room for this oyster girl and me
Where we may eat and drink and merry merry be
And have white bread and wine to our oysters.'

'O yes,' said the drawboy 'O yes,' said he
'I have got a room for the oyster girl and thee
Where you may eat and drink and merry merry be
And have white bread and wine to your oysters.'

They hadna been in there and long sitten down
When she's picked his pockets of five hundred pounds
She's pickèd his pockets and down the stairs did run
And left him with the creelie of oysters

He called for the drawboy, 'O drawboy,' said he
'Have you seen the oyster girl that I brought in with me?
For she's picked my pocket of five hundred pounds
And left me with her creelie of oysters.'

'O yes,' said the drawboy, 'O yes,' said he
'I saw the oyster girl that you brought in with thee
She's up yonder lane and she's over yonder lea
And she's learned you the way to buy oysters.'

'Then,' said the gentleman 'I'm not worth a groat.'
'O then,' said the drawboy 'I must have your coat.
Since you have got your neck into the yoke
For the white bread and wine to your oysters.'

O I've been in England and I've been in France
But never did I meet with such a mischance
A Scotch girl has learned an Englishman to dance
She's learned him the way to buy oysters.

THIS TALE, RESEMBLING Maggie May's, crops up all over the British Isles – here, in a set printed by Greig, at the expense of a prosperous Englishman in Scotland. Unlike Maggie May, the oyster girl gets away with it. The erotic significance of her oysters is undisguised.

The tune comes from the singing of Joe Saunders, Biggin Hill, Kent, recorded in 1967.

creelie: basket

ROUD #875

FRATRICIDE

The deliberate killing of a brother or sister – the legal term fratricide covers both – is murder like any other. But the murder of a sibling, almost always motivated by jealousy, has a psychological element which gives it a special place in ballad literature.

The songs in this section are some of the best known and most widely distributed, not only among Scots and English singers but in European folk song and story.

THE TWA SISTERS

A

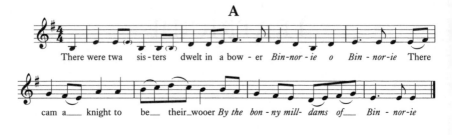

B

There were twa sisters dwelt in a bower
  Binnorie o Binnorie
There cam a knight to be their wooer
  By the bonny mill-dams of Binnorie

He courted the eldest wi' glove and ring
But he lo'ed the youngest aboon anything

He courted the eldest wi' brooch and knife
But he lo'ed the youngest aboon his life

The eldest she was vexèd sair
And envied sore her sister fair

The eldest to the youngest said
'Will you see our father's ships come in?'

She's ta'en her by the lily hand
And led her down to the river strand

The youngest stood upon a stane
The eldest cam and pushed her in

O sister, sister reach your hand
And ye'll be heir of half my land

'O sister, I'll not reach my hand
And I'll be heir of all your land

'O sister reach me but your glove
And sweet William shall be your love.'

'Sink on, nor hope for hand or glove
William shall better be my love

'Your cherry cheeks and yellow hair
Garred me gang maiden ever mair.'

Sometimes she sank, sometimes she swam
Until she cam to the miller's dam

The miller's daughter was baking breid
And gaed for water as she had need

O father, father draw your dam
There's either a mermaid or a milk-white swan

The miller hasted and drew his dam
And there he found a drown'd woman

Ye couldna see her yellow hair
For gowd and pearls that were sae rare

Ye couldna see her middle sma'
Her gowden girdle was sae braw

Ye couldna see her lily feet
Her gowden fringes were sae deep

There was a harper passing by
The sweet pale face he chanced to spy

And when he looked that lady on
He sighed and made a heavy moan

Sair will they be, whate'er they be
The hearts that live to weep for thee

He made a harp of her breast-bone
Whose sounds would melt a heart of stone

The strings he fram'd of her yellow hair
Their notes made sad the listening ear

He brought it to her father's ha'
There was the court assembled a'

He laid the harp upon a stane
And straight it 'gan to play alane

'O yonder sits my father the king
And yonder sits my mother the queen

And yonder stands my brother Hugh
And by him my William sweet and true.'

But the last tune that the harp played then
Was 'Woe to my sister, false Helen.'

IN THE MANY KNOWN versions – Child recorded twenty-one and Bronson added more – the unvarying theme is the drowning of the lovely younger sister by the jealous older one, and the harp or viol strung with the drowned girl's hair which finally sings out an accusation. Child traced the story in Scots, Irish, Welsh, English and many other northern European traditions.

The lyric used here is the one printed by Bruce and Stokoe in their *Northumbrian Minstrelsy*, which corresponds closely with the version in Scott's *The Minstrelsy of the Scottish Border*. This may account for some of the literary touches, but the lyric does not lend itself to patchwork. Bronson, however, detected 'rash confidence' in Bruce and Stokoe's claim that their previously unpublished tune (tune **A** here) is 'a true Northumbrian melody' which 'differs from the Scottish tune, which is of modern date'.

By the nineteenth century the song commonly accompanied a play-dance, particularly in the USA; but it is known to be of much greater antiquity, for there is evidence of a 1656 broadside version, and of book publication in 1658.

Tune **B** is an anonymous manuscript version held by one of the present editors, initialled 'H. T. 1946' and annotated:

> Tune still heard for a variant of 'Binnorie' given me by Miss K. M. Briggs. Miss Briggs described to me the action of this singing-game as played in Perthshire – 4 players – the brother 'burled' her round till the girl dropped to the ground. The brother finally kills himself v. realistically.

CHILD #10   ROUD #8

MY SON DAVIE

'Why does your brand sae drap wi bluid *My son Da-vie, o son Da-vie* Why does your brand sae drap. wi bluid *The truth come tell to__ me.'* 'It is the bluid o' my grey hawk *La-dy mi-ther, la-dy mi-ther* Tis the bluid o' my__ grey hawk *Be-cause she'd no be ruled by__ me.'*

'Why does your brand sae drap wi bluid
My son Davie, o son Davie
Why does your brand sae drap wi bluid
The truth come tell to me.'

'It is the bluid o' my grey hawk
Lady mither, lady mither
Tis the bluid o' my grey hawk
Because she'd no be ruled by me.'

'Thy hawk's bluid was ne'er sae red
My son Davie, o son Davie
They hawk's bluid was ne'er sae red
The truth come tell to me.'

'Tis the bluid o' my greyhound
Lady mither, lady mither
Tis the bluid o' my greyhound
Because she wadna run for me.'

'Thy hound's bluid was ne'er sae red
    My son Davie, o son Davie
Thy hound's bluid was ne'er sae red
    The truth come tell to me.'

'It is the bluid o' my brither John
    Lady mither, lady mither
Tis the bluid o' my brither John
    The truth I've told to thee.'

'About what did the fray begin?
    My son Davie, o son Davie
About what did the fray begin?
    The truth come tell to me.'

'The cutting of a willow wand
    Lady mither, lady mither
The cutting of a willow wand
When a penny wad hae bought the tree.'

'What death dost thou desire to die?
    My son Davie, o son Davie
What death dost thou desire to die?
    The truth come tell to me.'

'I'll set my foot in a bottomless ship
    Lady mither, lady mither
I'll set my foot in a bottomless ship
And ye'll never see mair o' me.'

THIS VERSION of one of the classic ballads (here without the parting curses placed by Davie on his family) uses the tune to which it was sung by the great Scots traditional singer and Traveller Jeannie Robertson. It combines her text and Motherwell's.

CHILD #13   ROUD #200

INFANTICIDE

It was becoming recognized by the mid-nineteenth century that the killing of a newborn child by its mother was not necessarily an act of malice or volition. Indeed, it ran counter to the Victorian understanding of nature and motherhood. So, long before the crime was reduced to the equivalent of manslaughter by the Infanticide Act of 1922, judges were sometimes steering juries not to convict where a mother was charged with murdering her newborn infant. This said, the concealment of unwanted births was endemic in a society in which the stigma of extramarital relations was indelible, and the deliberate killing of newborn babies, with its grim companion baby-farming, was correspondingly frequent.

The Infanticide Act defined the reduced offence as the killing of a child within twelve months of its birth when the balance of the mother's mind was still disturbed by the hormonal effects of childbirth or breastfeeding. The ballads do not show this modern understanding, but they do recognize the unnatural character of such a killing and the enduring remorse it brought.

MARY HAMILTON
(THE QUEEN'S THREE MARIES)

Word has tae— the kit-chen gane And word's gane tae the ha'___ That
Ma - ry Ham-il - ton gangs wi' bairn Tae the high - est Stew-art of a'

Word has tae the kitchen gane
And word's gane tae the ha'
That Mary Hamilton gangs wi' bairn
Tae the highest Stewart of a'

He's courted her in the kitchen
He's courted her in the ha'
He's courted her in the laigh cellar
And that was warst of a'

She's tied it in her apron
And thrown it in the sea
Saying, 'Sink ye, swim ye, bonny wee babe,
You'll get nae mair o' me.'

Down then cam the auld queen
Gowd tassels in her hair
'O Mary, where's the bonny wee babe
That I heard greet sae sair?'

'There is nae babe within my bower
I hope there ne'er will be
Twas but a touch o' my sair side
Cam o'er my fair bodie.'

'O Mary put on your robes o' black
Or else your robes o' brown
For ye maun gang wi' me the nicht
To see fair Edinbro town.'

'I winna put on my robes o' black
Nor yet my robes o' brown
But I'll put on my robes o' white
Tae shine thro Edinbro town.'

When she gaed up the Cannongate
She laughed loud laughters three
When she came down the Cannongate
The tear blinded her e'e

'O little did my mither think
When first she cradled me
What lands I was to travel through
What death I was to dee

'Last night I washed the queen's ain feet
And gently laid her down
And a' the thanks I've gotten the nicht
Tae be hanged in Edinbro toon

'Last nicht the queen had four Maries
The nicht she'll hae but three
There was Mary Seton and Mary Beaton
And Mary Carmichael and me.'

A SUBSTANTIAL AMOUNT of historical fact is woven into this ballad.

Mary Stuart as a child was sent to France in 1548 with four ladies-in-waiting, all named Mary, from the families of Seton, Beaton of Creich, Fleming and Livingston. There is no record of a Mary Hamilton in her entourage, nor of any of her ladies-in-waiting being executed for infanticide.

There was, however, a Mary Hamilton whose family married into the Russian aristocracy. She became a maid of honour to Catherine, the wife of Peter the Great, whose lover she became. When an infant's body was found wrapped in a court napkin, Mary confessed under torture to having borne and killed the child. She was executed wearing a white silk robe with black ribbons.

This was in 1719. It is possible that her name and much of the narrative detail was incorporated into an earlier Scots ballad of which no record survives; but it is likelier that the entire ballad – of which, as Child notes, there is no record prior to 1790 – originated in the eighteenth century, transposing Mary Hamilton's tragic story from Peter the Great's Russia to sixteenth-century Scotland.

This version of the text is taken principally from Sharpe's *Ballad Book* (1824), amplified by Child from manuscript sources. More than one tune has been associated with the words. The present one, probably the best known, was taken down by Gavin Greig from a Mrs Walker of Huntly (early collectors rarely felt it proper to ask or note their informants' full names) and published in 1925. A version of it, widespread in Perthshire, had been noted in the 1880s.

CHILD #173   ROUD #79

THE CRUEL MOTHER

She's sat down below a thorn
Fine flowers in the valley
And there she has her sweet babe born
And the green leaves they grow rarely

'Smile na sae sweet my bonny babe
Gin ye smile sae sweet ye'll smile me dead.'

She's ta'en out her little pen-knife
And twinned the sweet babe o' its life

She's howkit a grave by the licht o' the moon
And there she's buried her sweet babe in

As she was going tae the church
She saw a sweet babe in the porch

'O bonnie babe, gin ye were mine
I wad cleed thee in silk sae fine.'

'O mither dear when I was thine
Ye didna prove tae me sae kind.'

PRINCIPALLY BECAUSE broadside printers and song ped-
lars felt it necessary to moralize their tales, traditional song is
unforgiving. There is no sympathy, only remorse and condem-
nation, for the young woman characterized in the perennial
title of this ballad as a cruel mother.

The version given here, including its tune, comes from
Johnson's *Scots Musical Museum*.

cleed: dress

CHILD #20   ROUD #9

SEXUAL ASSAULT

There is a great deal of violence, much of it sexual, in traditional ballad and song. One genre of murder ballad begins with orthodox courtship followed by rape, and rape by murder. In some narratives the would-be rapist is thwarted. In others it becomes difficult to distinguish courtship from harassment or pursuit. In all such respects, folk song displays much the same ambivalence, much the same moralism and much the same hypocrisy as are encountered in modern societies.

One particularly unpleasant genre of traditional song celebrates wife-beating. Songs like 'The Wife Wrapt in a Wether's Skin' (so that her husband can deny beating her) and 'John Appleby' (who beats his wife into domestic submission), although printed without adverse comment by Greig and Williams respectively, find no place here. But this section does include a rarely heard song of courage and survival in the face of marital brutality, 'The Coat of Colours Three'.

THE BROOMFIELD WAGER

'A wa - ger, a wa - ger, a wa - ger I__ will lay__ Here's five hun-dred gui - neas to__ your ten__ That a mai - den you may go to the mer - ry green broom But__ a mai-den you shall ne - ver more re - turn.'

'A wager, a wager, a wager I will lay
Here's five hundred guineas to your ten
That a maiden you may go to the merry green broom
But a maiden you shall never more return.'

'I'll wager, I'll wager with you kind sir
It's your five hundred guineas to my ten
That a maiden I will go to the merry green broom
And a maiden I'll return back again.'

And when that she got to the bonny broom field
Her true love he was there fast asleep
With his horse and his hound and his fine silken gown
And his sword it lay down by his feet

Three times she did dance round the crown of his head
And three times around his feet
And three times she kissed his red cherry lips
As he lay on the ground fast asleep

She took from her left hand her diamond ring
And placed it on his right thumb
Saying, 'That's to be a token when he does awake
That his lady has been here and is gone.'

'O where were you, my good grey mare
That once I bought so dear
That you did not awaken me out of my sleep
When my true love was here?'

'I patted with my foot, master
And three times I made my bells to ring
And still I cried "Awake, master, awake
For now is the hour and the time."'

'Had I been awake when my true love was here
And had I not gainèd my will
All these wild birds on the merry broomfield
This night they should all have had their fill.'

THIS TEXT OF A disturbing and widespread ballad is taken principally from the set collected about the time of the Great War by Alfred Williams from Charles Tanner, 'an aged Morris dancer, of Bampton', collated with variants found by Sharp and Greig. Child has a number of striking Scots versions.

On one view the young woman has bewitched her would-be killer. On another, he has fallen victim to his own indolence and self-assurance. Either way, she has avoided a grim fate at his hands.

The tune given here is a variant of the tune taken down in 1907 by Cecil Sharp from Priscilla Cooper of Stafford Common.

CHILD #43   ROUD #34

MUST I BE BOUND?

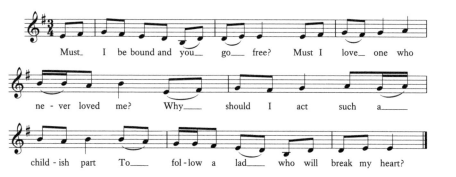

Must I be bound and you go free?
Must I love one who never loved me?
Why should I act such a childish part
To follow a lad who will break my heart?

The first thing that my lad gave me
It was a cap well lined with lead
And the longer that I wore that cap
It grew the heavier on my head

And next he brought me a gown to wear
Lined with sorrow, stitched with care
And the drink he gave me was bitter gall
And the blows he gave me were worse than all

The third thing that my lad gave me
It was a belt of colours three
The first was shame, the next was sorrow
And last of all sad misery

But I shall climb a higher tree
And I shall find a richer nest
And I'll come down and shall not fall
And marry a lad I may love best.

VERY FEW FOLK songs deal honestly with male domestic violence, and far too many treat it as a subject of mirth. This song is a rarity both in its realism and in the courage it portrays.

The present version, taken from the collated version in *The Seeds of Love*, is based on a diffuse text in Sam Henry's Northern Ireland collection and another in Christie's *Traditional Ballad Airs*.

The tune, which comes from Henry's alphabetical notation, will have been sent to him by one of his correspondents.

ROUD #18829

THE TWA MAGICIANS

The lady stands in her bower door
Straight as a willow wand
The blacksmith stood a little forbye
Wi' a hammer in his hand
Wi' a hammer in his hand

'Weel may ye dress ye, lady fair
Intae your robes o' red
Before the morn at this same time
I'll gain your maidenhead.'

'Awa' awa' ye coal-black smith
Would you do me the wrang
To think to gain my maidenhead
That I hae kept sae lang.'

Then she became a turtle dow
To fly up in the air

And he became another dow
And they flew pair and pair

She turned herself into an eel
To swim intae yon burn
And he became a speckled trout
To gie the eel a turn

She turned hersel' into a hare
To rin upon yon hill
And he became a gude greyhound
And boldly he did fill

Then she became a gay grey mare
And stood in yonder slack
And he became a gilt saddle
And sat upon her back

She turned herself into a ship
To sail out ower the flood
He ca'ed a nail intill her tail
And syne the ship she stood

Then she became a silken plaid
And stretched upon a bed
And he became a green covering
And gained her maidenhead.

THE SCOTTISH TEXT of this magical ballad was to be found, alone and tuneless, in Buchan's *Ballads of the North of Scotland* (1828), until in 1904 a Somerset blacksmith (appropriately named Sparks) sang to Cecil Sharp what was clearly an English version of the song in 6/8 time ('The Two Magicians').

Rather than attempt a forced marriage of the two, the present version sets Buchan's lyric to a tune associated with the strikingly similar opening verse of 'The Gardener':

> Proud Maisrie stands in her bower door
> Straight as a willow wand
> And by it comes a gardener lad
> Wi' a red rose in his hand

In spite of the ferocity of the pursuit, the culmination is gentle, perhaps even consensual.

forbye: distant   **slack:** morass; alt.
leman: lover   narrow pass
dow: dove   **syne:** then
fill: follow, pursue   **ca'd (called):** drove

CHILD #44   ROUD #135

BOGIE'S BONNY BELLE

As I gaed doon tae Huntly toon
The market for tae fee
I met Bogheid o' Cairnie
And wi' him I did agree

Tae work his twa best horses
On barrow, cart or plough
And anything about the farm
I very well could do

Now Bogie was a greedy man
And I did know it well
But Bogie had a daughter
Her name was Isabelle

And Belle she was the bonniest lass
In all the countryside
And very soon I lost my heart
Tae the belle of Bogieside

Now when she went out walking
She took me for her guide

Down by the burn of Cairnie
Tae see the fishes glide

I slipped my arms around her waist
Her feet frae her did slide
And it's there I've ta'en my will of her
Down by the Bogieside

When nine lang months were past and gone
She brought me forth a son
And I was quickly sent for
To see what could be done

I said that I would marry her
But oh, that wouldna dae
Saying you're nae match for Bogie's Belle
And she's nae match for thee

And now she's married wi' a tinker lad
And they bide in Huntly toon
And with pots and pans and Tilley lamps
He scours the country round

Maybe she's got her a better match
Good faith, I canna tell
But 'twas me that took the maidenhead
Of Bogie's bonny Belle.

THE BURN OF CAIRNIE is a tributary of the River Isla, a few miles northwest of Huntly in Aberdeenshire. Bogie or Boghead is likely to have been the name of the farmer's estate. Gavin Greig, early in the twentieth century, noted information that had reached him that the song had been composed 54 years earlier by the foreman at Boghead of Cairnie, John Geddes.

Thanks to research in the local parish and census records by the Aberdeen singer and scholar Peter Hall (1936–1996), it is probable that Belle was Isabel Morison, born at Boghead in September 1823, the daughter of Alexander Morison. Her son James was born in June 1843, when she was not quite twenty. The father was registered as James Stephen, evidently the ploughman-narrator. By the time of the 1851 census, Isabel was no longer at Boghead (very possibly because she had married) and her son James was living with the ploughman's brother in a neighbouring parish.

'Bogie's Bonny Belle' is one of the most touching ballads in the traditional Scots repertoire. The ploughman narrator admits to what is, at least to any modern understanding, a rape. When a son is born he makes no attempt to deny his paternity, but his offer to make amends by marriage is rebuffed – in most versions on the ground that Belle is socially too good for him. If so, her father is making a bad mistake: with a child born out of wedlock she will be all but unmarriageable within his community. And so it proves.

In at least one version, however, the family demand that the ploughman should marry her and he refuses. In another variant, he takes the child away (which seems to have been what actually happened). As to Belle's consequent fall from social acceptance, the ploughman cannot resist a bitter jibe in the final verse: by rejecting his offer of marriage, it is the farmer who has ruined his daughter's life. As ever, it is Belle who suffers the penalty.

Variants of the ballad are widespread within and beyond the Scottish Traveller community. While the words are first found in print in the early twentieth century, the text given here draws on the versions sung by Jane Stewart, Davy Stewart and Winnie Campbell.

There are some graphic variants. In some, 'he', in the final line of the penultimate verse becomes 'they' or even 'she', making Belle a travelling tinker.

But the bruising final couplet taken here from the singing of the Perthshire Traveller Jane Stewart is more often:

> Fareweel ye lads o' Huntly toon
> And Bogie's bonny Belle.

The tune, simple and lovely, rarely varies.

In practically all recorded versions the first vowel in 'Isabel' is a long 'I'.

The market for tae fee: the feeing market was where farmers hired labour for the coming year.

ROUD #2155

ABDUCTION

Abduction is not a distinct crime, but forcibly carrying a person away almost invariably amounts to the common-law offences of assault and false imprisonment. Abduction for sexual or marital purposes has for centuries been a serious crime, and in ecclesiastical law coercion rendered a marriage void.

The doctrine of the English common law that a woman consents in advance to sexual relations with her husband was not reversed by the English courts until 1991. Two years earlier the Scottish high court held that this had never been the law of Scotland. That marriage cannot be a defence to rape is now confirmed by statute, and carrying off or detaining a woman to force her to marry has since 1956 been a statutory crime.

By contrast, Sir Walter Scott quotes 'a respectable woman' who reacted to his censure of the McGregor clan by asserting 'that there was no use in giving a bride too much choice upon such occasions; that the marriages were happiest lang syne which had been done off hand . . . and that her own mother had never seen her father till the night he brought her up from the Lennox with ten head of black cattle, and there had not been a happier couple in the country.'

The ballads in any case show little interest in legalities. Eppie Morrie fights off a man who, having put her through a forced marriage ceremony, tries but fails to exercise what was regarded as his conjugal right. Jean Key fails to hold off Rob Roy in a similar situation; but the ballad is less concerned with her distress than with his virility.

The only grim certainty is the hanging of the Gypsies whose singing has seduced the wife of the Earl of Cassilis.

EPPIE MORRIE

Four and twen-ty Hie-land men— Cam frae the Car-ron side To steal a-wa' Ep-pie Mor-rie For she wad-na be a bride *A bride She wad-na be a bride*

Four and twenty Hieland men
Cam frae the Carron side
To steal awa' Eppie Morrie
For she wadna be a bride
   A bride
   She wadna be a bride

Out it cam her mither
It was a moonlicht nicht
She couldna see her daughter
For the waters shone sae bricht

Haud awa' frae me, mother
Far awa' frae me
There's no a man in a' Strathdon
Shall wedded be with me

They've taken Eppie Morrie then
And a horseback bound her on
And then awa' to the minister
As fast as horse could gang

Then Willie's ta'en his pistol out
Set it to the minister's breast
'Marry me, marry me, minister
Or else I'll be your priest.'

'Haud awa' frae me, good sir
Haud awa' frae me
I daurna avow to marry you
Except she's willing as ye.'

'Haud far awa' frae me, Willie
Haud awa' frae me
There's not a man in a' Strathdon
Shall wedded be with me.'

They've ta'en Eppie Morrie then
Since better couldna be
And they're awa' to Carrie side
As fast as horse could flee

When mass was sung and bells were rung
And all were bound for bed
Then Willie and Eppie Morrie
In ane bed they were laid

He's ta'en the sark frae off his back
And kicked awa' his shoon
And thrown awa' the chaumer key
And naked he lay doon

'Haud awa' frae me, Willie
Haud awa' frae me
Before I'll lose my maidenhead
I'll try my strength wi' thee.'

She took the cap frae off her head
And threw it to the way
Saying, 'Ere I lose my maidenhead
I'll fight wi' you till day.'

He's kissed her on the lily breast
And held her shoulders twa
But aye she grat and aye she spat
And turnèd to the wa'

And through the nicht they warsled there
Until the licht of day
And Willie grat and Willie swat
But he couldna stretch her spey

Then early in the morning
Before her clothes were on
In cam the maid o' Scallater
Wi' gown and shirt alane

'Get up, get up, young woman
And drink the wine with me.'
'Ye might ha' ca'd me maiden
For I'm sure as leal as thee.'

'Weary fa' ye, Willy, then
That ye coudna prove a man
And ta'en the lassie's maidenhead
She wad have hired your hand.'

'Go get for me a horse, Willie
And get it like a man
And send me back to my mither
A maiden as I cam.

'The sun shines o'er the westlin hills
By the lamplicht o' the moon
Come saddle your horse, young John Forsyth
And whistle and I'll come soon.'

THERE IS A SINGLE received text to this ballad, printed in 1824 in James Maidment's *North Countrie Garland* without a tune; but it was evidently known to Walter Scott, who in *Rob Roy* quoted what appear to be its first two verses. Maidment's text ends with a clear echo of Robert Burns's poem 'Whistle and I'll Come to You, My Lad'.

'Morrie', a surname not encountered elsewhere, may be a variant of Murray or Moray. Loch Carron is on the west coast of Scotland, while the village of Carron is in the northeast, near Aberlour. Strathdon is an area of Aberdeenshire on the river Don.

In the early 1950s, Alan Lomax recorded a sung version of the ballad from the Scots Traveller Jimmy MacBeath. By then it had entered the repertoire of the folk revival through

Ewan MacColl, who attributed it to his father, William Miller of Stirling, and his father's friend Samuel Wylie of Falkirk. It is probable that this was MacBeath's source. It is also likely that the tune was the work of MacColl himself, who had a fine ear and was eminently capable of fusing tradition with composition. In fact the tenth, thirteenth and fourteenth verses given here have no analogue in Maidment's text. They may well be MacColl's (see *The Singing Island*, pp. 15, 109) but they are too good to omit. So is the inspired use of moonlit waters in the second verse where Maidment, more logically but more prosaically, has swords glinting in the moonlight.

Bronson at all events considered MacColl's version 'embedded in the folk tradition', citing the similarity of 'the triadic alternation of the first two phrases between tonic minor and tonic major' to the first strain of another ballad, 'The Piper of Dundee'. It is used here not for want of an alternative but as a handsome vehicle for a fine ballad.

The lyric, which has an undoubted feel of authenticity, recounts and celebrates the determination of a young woman to fight off a husband who has been forced on her. As the ballad ends, she sets off to find her real lover, John Forsyth. This has meant omitting a dramatic but incompatible verse from MacColl's version in which, out of the blue, an armed rescuer arrives.

chaumer: chamber   **westlin:** western
grat: scratched   **swat:** sweated
to the way: ? at the wall   **spey:** hymen
haud awa': keep off   **leal:** chaste
daurna: dare not

CHILD #223   ROUD #2583

ROB ROY

Rob Roy frae the Hie- lands cam And to_ the_ Low- land bor - der It
was_ to_ steal a_ fair_ la - dy To_ hold his_ house in_ or - der

2nd strain
'Be con -tent, be con-tent Be con-tent with me, la - dy Now you are my
wed-ded wife Un - til the day you die, la - dy. 'Rob Roy was my fa -ther and Mc-
Greg - or was his name, la - dy All the coun - try
far and near Have heard Mc - Gre - gor's fame, la - dy'

Rob Roy frae the Hielands cam
And to the Lowland border
It was to steal a fair lady
To hold his house in order

And he has ta'en Jean Key's white hand
And torn her grass-green sleeve
And roughly tied her on his horse
And asked her friends nae leave

'I winna go with you,' she says
'I winna be your honey
I winna be your wedded wife
You love me for my money.'

They rode till they cam to Ballyshine
At Ballyshine they tarried
There he bought her cloak and gown
But she would not be married

Three held her up before the priest
Four carried her to bed-o
So mournfully she wept and cried
When she by him was laid-o

   'Be content, be content
   Be content with me, lady
   Now you are my wedded wife
   Until the day you die, lady

'Rob Roy was my father and
McGregor was his name, lady
All the country far and near
Have heard McGregor's fame, lady

   'Be content, be content
   Be content wi' me, lady
   Whare'll ye find in Lennox land
   Sae braw a man as me, lady?

'My father he has cows and ewes
He has goats and sheep, lady
You and twenty thousand pounds
Mak me a man complete, lady

'I'm as bold, I'm as bold
I'm as bold and more, lady
Any man that doubts my word
Shall feel my good claymore, lady

'Be content, be content
Be content to stay, lady
Never think of going back
Until your dying day, lady.'

ROB ROY (actually Robert Oig, meaning junior) MacGregor was the youngest of the five sons of Walter Scott's eponymous hero. With a youthful reputation for violence, he was outlawed in 1736, enlisted in the British army, was wounded and captured at Fontenoy in 1745, and was returned to Scotland by way of an exchange. There he married into a respectable family but, widowed within a few years, decided with the encouragement of his brother James to adopt the MacGregor family practice of wife-abduction.

Jean Key, still only nineteen, had been widowed and reputedly left wealthy. On the night of 8 December 1750, the MacGregors laid siege to her family home, dragged her out, carried her by horse to Buchanan and then by water to near Loch Lomond. After more than three months' captivity, she was taken before a minister at or near Rowerdennan, who declared her and Rob Oig man and wife.

Here the ballad ends, but the MacGregors were forced to release Jean. Two years later James was convicted of hamesucken (invasion of a private house) and forcible abduction, but escaped from Edinburgh Castle. Rob was less fortunate: a year later he was arrested and tried. In spite of Jean's evidence that he had relented but had been intimidated by his brother James into continuing with the abduction, he was convicted and in February 1754 was hanged.

The text given here is a composite version based on the Pitcairn manuscript (Child variant E). An unusual feature of the ballad, occurring in three of Child's variants, is the change of tune midway. The first strain, following Motherwell's and Pitcairn's indications, is associated with both 'Gipsy Laddie' and 'The Bonny House o' Airlie'. The second strain is identified by both Pitcairn and Motherwell as 'Haud Awa Frae Me, Donald', and is taken here from a version in Greig's manuscripts.

> **claymore:** 'a large sword formerly used by the Scottish Highlanders . . . now applied inaccurately to the baskethilted sword of the officers of Highland regiments' (Chambers Dictionary).

CHILD #225   ROUD #340

THE GREY SELCHIE OF SULE SKERRY

An earth-ly nour-rice sits and sings And aye she sings, 'Ba li-ly wean___

Lit-tle ken I my bair-nie's fa-ther Far___ less the land that he stops in.'

An earthly nourrice sits and sings
And aye she sings, 'Ba lily wean
Little ken I my bairnie's father
Far less the land that he stops in.'

Then ane arose at her bed-foot
And a grimly guest for sure was he
Saying, 'Here am I, thy bairnie's father
Although that I be not comely

'I am a man upon the land
And I am a selchie in the sea
And when I'm far and far frae land
My dwelling is in Sule Skerry.'

'It wasna weel,' quoth the maiden fair
'It wasna weel indeed,' quo' she
'That the grey selchie of Sule Skerry
Should hae come and aught a bairn to me.'

Now he has ta'en a purse o' gowd
And he has pit it on her knee

Saying, 'Gie tae me my little young son
And tak thee up thy nourrice fee

'And it sall pass on a simmer's day
When the sun shines het on every stane
That I will tak my little young son
And teach him for to swim the faem

'And thou sall marry a proud gunner
And a proud gunner I'm sure he'll be
And the very first shot that e'er he shoots
He'll shoot baith my young son and me.'

SULE SKERRY IS a remote island off the north coast of Scotland.

Sea-creatures, often seals, which can adopt and abandon human form are well-known in Nordic mythology. The poignancy of this ballad lies in the return of the grey seal (in some versions the 'great seal'), who has fathered a human son, to take him to a foreordained death at human hands.

The text was found by Child in a single variant taken down by a naval captain 'from the dictation of a venerable lady of Snarra Voe, Shetland' and published, tuneless, by the Society of Antiquaries of Scotland in 1852.

The words have been set in recent times to a handsome composed tune that has given the ballad new life. But the original ballad had in fact survived in oral tradition: it was recorded in 1938, with the tune given here, from John Sinclair, a fisherman and farmer, of Flotta in the Orkneys, who had learnt it from his mother.

aught a bairn: give a child

ba lily wean: lullaby

nourrice: wet-nurse

selchie: seal

faem: foam

CHILD #113   ROUD #197

THE GYPSY LADDIES

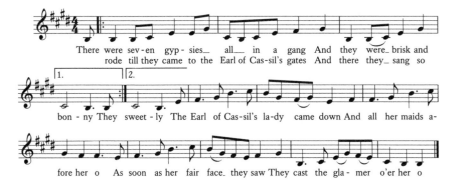

There were sev-en gyp-sies_ all_ in a gang And they were_ brisk and
rode till they came to the Earl of Cas-sil's gates And there they_ sang so

bon - ny They sweet-ly The Earl of Cas-sil's la-dy came down And all her maids a-

fore her o As soon as her fair face_ they saw They cast the gla - mer o'er her o

There were seven gipsies all in a gang
And they were brisk and bonny
They rode till they came to the
    Earl of Cassil's gates
And there they sang so sweetly
The Earl of Cassil's lady came down
And all her maids afore her o
As soon as her fair face they saw
They cast the glamer o'er her o

They gave to her a nutmeg brown
They gave to her the ginger
She gave to them a far better thing
The gold ring off her finger
She pulled off her high heeled shoes
Made of Spanish leather o
And she put on her highland brogues
To follow the gypsy laddie o

At night when her good lord cam hame
And asking for his lady o
Some they cried and others they replied
She's awa' with the gipsy laddie o
'Come saddle me my milk-white steed
The black rides not so speedy o
For I will neither eat nor sleep
Till I have found my lady o.'

He rode all the summer's night
And part of the next morning
Until he spied his own wedded wife
She was cold and wet and weary
'Last night I lay in a well-made bed
With my good lord beside me o
Tonight I will lie in the open fields
Along with the gipsy laddie o.'

'Come home, come home, my own wedded wife
It's get thee on behind me
And I will swear by the handle of my sword
That a gipsy never will come nigh thee.'
'O I have lain on the grass so green
And I have drank o' the heather o
And as I brew so will I bake
And I'll follow my gipsy for ever o.'

Seven gipsies all in a gang
Black but they were bonny
And they were hangèd all in a row
For stealing the Earl of Cassil's lady.

IN 1541, A YEAR after James V had recognized the Gypsy chieftain Johnnie Faa as 'Lord and Earl of Little Egypt', his council expelled all Gypsies from the realm on pain of death. The Scottish parliament again expelled them in 1609. Hangings of groups of Gypsies for the crime of remaining or returning followed in 1611, 1616 and 1624. The last of these was a group consisting of Johnnie Faa and seven others; eleven of their womenfolk were sentenced to be drowned but were reprieved.

In the course of the eighteenth century, legend began to attribute these hangings to the seduction, or abduction, of the wife of the Earl of Cassilis. In the earl's absence in London, the story went, Sir John Faa, with whom the countess had once been in love, returned to the Cassilis seat at Maybole in Ayrshire with a group of fellow Gypsies and sang to her at the castle gates, luring her out. The countess was subsequently confined to a newly built turret on which the heads of her eight seducers were carved in effigy.

Notwithstanding its distinctively Scots features and Gavin Greig's numerous findings of it in Aberdeenshire, the ballad was found by Sam Henry in Ireland and by Baring-Gould in Devon. It remains current among English and Scots Travellers. The text used here is collated from Child and Sam Henry. The tune, a relative of the 'Geordie' group, is adapted from Smith's *Scottish Minstrel*.

glamer: spell, charm

CHILD #200   ROUD #1

TRANSPORTATION

The use of the criminal justice system to provide forced labour for Britain's new colonies was first authorized by a statute of 1597. Prisoners under sentence of death would be offered a reprieve in return for agreeing to be transported, usually to the American colonies, for a fixed period of either penal servitude or indentured labour, both akin to a state of slavery.

From 1717, transportation for a fixed term or for life became a distinct legal punishment. Following the closure of the American penal colonies, the first convict ship reached New South Wales in 1788. By the 1830s, the number of transported convicts exceeded 4,000 a year.

The hardships of the voyage, and then of years of forced labour in inhuman conditions, have been described by many historians, and they loom large in folk song. The broadside ballads composed by printers' hacks put penitential words into the offender's mouth to warn others of what lay in store for them. But transportation needed no preaching or exaggeration: the truth was quite bad enough.

Nevertheless, some transported convicts gained emancipation and settled as farmers. With the arrival of assisted migration, punitive transportation (save for a time to Western Australia) was brought to an end in 1853 and replaced by the scarcely less cruel punishment of penal servitude. By then, thousands of men and women had been forcibly shipped to Botany Bay and Van Diemen's Land, and many had never returned.

ADIEU TO ALL JUDGES AND JURIES

Here's a-dieu to all jud-ges and ju- ries___ Jus-tice and Old Bai-ley too Sev-en years they've sent me from my true love Sev-en years I'm_ trans-por-ted you know

Here's adieu to all judges and juries
Justice and Old Bailey too
Seven years they've sent me from my true love
Seven years I'm transported you know

To go to a strange country don't grieve me
Nor leaving old England behind
It's all for the sake of my Polly
And leaving my parents behind

How hard is the place of confinement
That keeps me from my heart's delight
Cold chains and cold irons surround me
And a plank for my pillow at night

Oh if I had the wings of an eagle
High up on those pinions I'd fly
I'd fly to the arms of my true love
And on her soft bosom I'd lie

If e'er I return from the ocean
Stores of riches I'll bring for my dear

And all for the sake of my true love
I will cross the salt seas without fear

Here's adieu to all judges and juries
Justice and Old Bailey too
Seven years they've sent me from my true love
Seven years I'm transported you know.

THIS IS A COLLATION of a broadside printed by Harkness of Preston, circa 1840, with the more lyrical version sung by Martin Carthy (which is put in the mouth not of the convict, as here, but of his lover).

The tune is a variant of the version sung to the composer Percy Merrick by his dependable informant Henry Hills of Lodsworth in West Sussex.

ROUD #300

VAN DIEMEN'S LAND

Come all you gal-lant poa - chers that ram- ble_free from care That walk out on a moon-lit night with your dog and_ gun and snare The harm-less hare and phea-sant you_ have at your com-mand Not think-ing of your last car-eer up - on Van_ Diem-en's land

Come all you gallant poachers that ramble free from
  care
That walk out on a moonlit night with your dog and
  gun and snare
The harmless hare and pheasant you have at your
  command
Not thinking of your last career upon Van Diemen's
  land

There was Tom Brown from Nottingham, Jack
  Williams and poor Joe
We were three daring poachers as the country well
  did know
At night we were trepanned by the keepers hid
  in sand
And for fourteen years transported unto Van
  Diemen's land

O when we sailed from England and landed at the
    bay
We had rotten straw for bedding, we dared not say
    them nay
Our cots are fenced with wire, we slumber when we
    can
And drive away the tigers upon Van Diemen's Land

The first day we were landed upon that fatal shore
The planters they came flocking, full twenty score or
    more
They ranked us up like horses, they sold us out of
    hand
And they yoked us to the plough, my boys, to plough
    Van Diemen's Land

There was a girl from England, Susan Somers was her
    name
For fourteen years transported, from London town
    she came
Our planter bought her freedom and married her out
    of hand
And she gave us all good usage upon Van Diemen's
    Land

Come all you gallant poachers, give ear unto my song
I'll give to you some good advice although it is not
    long
Lay by your dog and gun and snare, to you I will
    speak plain

If you knew the hardships we endure you'd never
poach again.

FROM THE SINGING of Joe Saunders, Biggin Hill, Kent, 1966.
The song is as widespread in Scotland as it is in England,
with Nottingham and London replaced by Glasgow, and with
a frequent final verse:

> Although the poor of Scotland do labour and
>   do toil
> They're robbed of every blessing and produce
>   of the soil
> Your proud imperious landlords, if you break
>   their command
> They'll send you to the British hulks or to Van
>   Diemen's Land.

trepanned: the older meaning of trepan was a snare or
a trap
tigers: the Tasmanian tiger, a species of wild dog long
since hunted to extinction, was real enough to the first
convicts

ROUD #519

ALL ROUND MY HAT

All round my hat I will wear the green wil-low   All round my hat for a twelve-month and__ a day   And if an-y-one should ask you   The rea-son I am wea-ring it It's all be-cause my__ true love is far far a-way

All round my hat I will wear the green willow
All round my hat for a twelvemonth and a day
And if anyone should ask you
The reason I am wearing it
It's all because my true love is far far away

My love she was fair and my love she was gentle
And cruel was the judge that my love had to try
For thieving was a thing she never was inclined to
But he sent my love across the seas and far far away

Seven long years my love and I are parted
Seven long years my love is bound to stay
Bad luck to any chap who would ever be false-hearted
I'll love her for ever though she's far away

There is some young men as is cruel and deceitful
A-coaxing of young girls they mean to lead astray
As soon as they deceive them, so cruelly they leave them
And never sighs nor sorrows when they're sent far away

I bought my love a ring on the very day she started
I gave it as a token for to remember me
And when she does come back we'll never more
   be parted
We'll marry and be happy for ever and a day

THIS SONG IS PART of the large body of Victorian burlesque, a parodic form of sentimental stage song, which adopts a tear-jerking storyline but overdoes it. 'Villikins and His Dinah' is one of the best-known examples. Thus 'All Round My Hat' was commonly performed with a pause every couple of lines for costermonger's patter: ''Ere's yer 'eads of celery . . . 'Ard 'earted cabbages . . .'.

The song comes through oral transmission in many variants, including several American ones which naturally make no mention of transportation as the cause of parting. Some broadsides give the tune as 'The Fisherman's Boy'. The radio writer and producer Charles Chilton, who was born in London in 1917 and who knew the song and its patter from oral tradition, sang it in 3/4 time.

ROUD #22518

BOTANY BAY

Come all young men of learning
A warning take by me
I'd have you quit night-walking
And shun bad company
I'd have you quit night-walking
Or else you'll rue the day
When you have been transported
And sent to Botany Bay

I was brought up in London
A place I know full well
Brought up by honest parents
The truth to you I'll tell
Brought up by honest parents
And reared so tenderly
Till I became a roving blade
Which proved my destiny

My character was taken
And I was sent to jail
My friends they tried to clear me
But nothing could prevail
At the Old Bailey sessions
The judge to me did say
'The jury's found you guilty
You must go to Botany Bay.'

As we sailed down the river
On the twenty-eighth of May
On every ship we passed
We heard the sailors say
'There goes a ship of clever lads
We're sorry for to say
They've done some crime or other
And they're bound for Botany Bay.'

OF THE MANY PRINTED and sung versions, the present text comes from the broadside source reproduced by Ashton (1888), shorn of two verses of excruciating sentimentality.

The tune is from the singing of Joe Saunders, Biggin Hill, recorded in 1967.

ROUD #5478

PRISON

For centuries prisons were privately or municipally run dungeons in which accused persons were held for interrogation, trial or execution.

It was principally under the pressure to reduce the use of the gallows and the temporary interruption of transportation to the colonies during the American War of Independence that the use of incarceration as a punishment developed. Much of the nineteenth century was spent in centralizing and standardizing the prison regimes.

From the 1770s, local prisons, used chiefly to hold prisoners facing felony charges, began to be used for shorter sentences of penal detention, and 'hulks' – moored ex-naval vessels – used for felons awaiting transportation. In 1816, the first, and for a long time the only, national penitentiary was opened on London's Millbank. It was followed in 1838 by Parkhurst on the Isle of Wight, intended initially to house juveniles sentenced to transportation.

From 1853, when the Penal Servitude Act replaced transportation with hard labour, the Victorians saw to it that prison was a grim experience. Hard labour, until its abolition in 1948, was gruelling, food was minimal and the cruel 'separate and silent' regime of enforced isolation – built into the design first of Pentonville, opened in 1842, and then of over fifty local prisons – drove many prisoners to, and often beyond, the brink of insanity (though the 'Treadmill Song' at least suggests a daily visit by the prison doctor, which is more than prisoners get now). It was not until late in the nineteenth century that imprisonment came to be regarded as an opportunity to educate and reform, a change which had been advocated by Quaker critics of the system for many years.

Prison was also used for indefinite incarceration for civil debt, real or alleged. Of the many debtors' prisons, the most famous was the London Clink, which, with its gate in Stoney Street, has entered the English language. Both Sharp and Gardiner collected a song, 'I Kept a Pack of Hounds', about a once wealthy man gaoled for civil debt. The practice was halted under the Commonwealth in 1649, but like all such reforms was reversed at the Restoration in 1660. It continued well into the twentieth century: in 1905 alone, over 11,000 civil debtors were gaoled.

I WISH THERE WEREN'T NO PRISONS

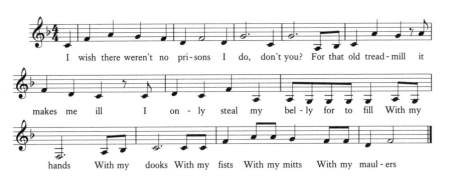

I wish there weren't no prisons
I do, don't you?
For that old treadmill it makes me ill
I only steal my belly for to fill
With my hands
With my dooks
With my fists
With my mitts
With my maulers.

I met a lady with a p'rambulator
She had two kiddies and each had a 'tater
In his hands
In his mitts
In his maulers
So I kissed one kiddie and I nicked the other's 'tater
With my hands
With my mitts
With my maulers

I wish there weren't no prisons
I do, don't you?
Cos this oakum picking
It makes me sicken
I got put in the gaol for nicking
With my hands
With my mitts
With my maulers

THE SONG 'DIXIE', composed in the 1850s by Daniel Emmett as a blackface minstrel number, was a colossal hit on both sides of the Atlantic. In the Civil War the song, with its show of nostalgia for the South, became the unofficial anthem of the Confederate states:

I wish I was in Dixie
Hooray! Hooray!
In Dixie land I'll take my stand
To live and die in Dixie
Away, away
To live and die in Dixie

One of the tune's attractions is that it provides a matrix into which almost any rhyming words can be fitted. The present song is one of dozens of examples: rather than score it, you take the melody and metre and either shoehorn or expand the words into them.

This version was recorded from Joe Saunders on Biggin Hill, Kent, in 1966.

dooks (or dukes), mitts, maulers: hands

ROUD #1708

THE TREADMILL SONG

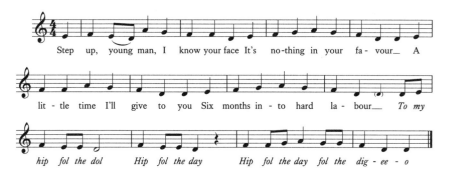

Step up, young man, I know your face It's no-thing in your fa - vour__ A
lit - tle time I'll give to you Six months in - to hard la - bour__ To my
hip fol the dol Hip fol the day Hip fol the day fol the dig - ee - o

Step up, young man, I know your face
It's nothing in your favour
A little time I'll give to you
Six months into hard labour

To my hip fol the dol
Hip fol the day
Hip fol the day fol the dig-ee-o

At six o'clock the turnkey comes
A bunch of keys all in his hand
Come on you lads, step up and grind
And tread the wheel till breakfast time

At eight o'clock our skilly comes in
Sometimes thick and sometimes thin
And if one word we chance to say
It's bread and water all next day

At half past eight the bell will ring
And to the chapel we must swing
There on our bended knees we fall
The Lord have mercy on us all

At nine o'clock the bell does ring
And to the trap, boys, we must spring
Come pray, my lads, to be on time
The wheel to tread and the corn to grind

At ten o'clock the doctor comes round
With a pen and paper in his hand
And if we say we are not ill
It's all next day the treading mill

Now Saturday's come and I'm sorry to say
Sunday is our starvation day
Our tin plates and our goblets too
They are not polished and they will not do

Now six long months is gone and past
And I'll return to my girl at last
I'll leave the turnkeys here behind
The wheel to tread and the corn to grind.

HENRY HAMMOND collected this song in 1906 from William Davey, an inmate of the Beaminster workhouse in Dorset – minus the verse about the Sunday food. This features on the version recorded by Ewan MacColl, who, however, omits the verse about the daily visit of a prison doctor authorized to issue sick-notes.

The tune is Davey's, transcribed from Hammond's manuscript by Frank Purslow in *Marrowbones*.

ROUD #1077

YOUNG BEICHAN (LORD BATEMAN)

In London city was Beichan born
He longed strange countries for to see
But he was ta'en by a savage Moor
Who handled him right cruelly

For through his shoulder he put a bore
And through the bore has pitten a tree
And he's gart him draw the carts of wine
Where horse and oxen had wont to be

He's casten him in a dungeon deep
Where he could neither hear nor see
He's shut him in a prison strong
And handled him right cruelly

'My hounds they all go masterless
My hawks they fly from tree to tree
My young brother will heir my land
Fair England more I'll never see

'Gin a lady would borrow me
It's at her foot that I would run

If a widow would borrow me
I would become her son.'

This Moor he had but one daughter
A fairer one you ne'er did see
And she stole the keys of her father's prison
And said she'd set Lord Beichan free

'O have you any lands?' she said
'Or castles in your own countrie
That ye would give to a lady fair
From prison strang to set you free?'

'O I have houses and I have lands
Northumberland belongs to me
I'll give them all to the lady fair
That out of prison will set me free.'

'Seven long years we'll make a vow
Seven long years we'll keep it strang
If you will wed no other woman
It's I will wed no other man

'Now set your foot on good shipboard
And haste ye back to your ain countrie
And before that seven years have an end
Come back again and marry me.'

But long ere seven years had an end
She longed again her love to see

For ever a voice within her breast
Said 'Beichan has broke his vow to thee.'

She sailèd east, she sailèd west
Till to fair England's shore she came
And a bonny shepherd lad she spied
Feeding his sheep upon the plain

'What news, what news, thou shepherd lad
What news hast thou to tell to me?'
'Such news, such news I hear, lady
The like was ne'er in this countrie

'There is a wedding in yonder hall
Has lasted these thirty days and three
For Beichan will not bed wi' his bride
For love of one beyond the sea.'

When she came to Lord Beichan's gate
She tirled softly at the pin
So ready was the proud porter
To open and let this lady in

When the porter came his lord before
He's knelt down low upon his knee
'There stands a lady at your gates
The like of whom I ne'er did see

For on every finger she has a ring
And on her mid-finger she has three

And so mickle gold above her brow
An earldom it would buy for me.'

Then quickly hied he down the stair
Of fifteen steps he made but three
He's ta'en his bonny love in his arms
And kissed and kissed her tenderly

She's lookit o'er her left shoulder
To hide the tears stood in her e'e
'Now fare thee well young Beichan,' she says
'I'll try to think nae more on thee.'

'Take back your daughter, madam,' he says
'And a double dowry I'll send her wi'
For I maun wed my first true love
That's done and suffered so much for me.'

THE STORY OF Lord Bateman, or Beichan, had an extraordinary distribution and durability. Child found numerous versions, both in manuscripts and on printed broadsides ('stall copies' he called them), one of which he 'picked off an old wall in Piccadilly' and collated with other sets.

The tale itself seems to originate in the eleventh century: Gilbert Becket, the father of Thomas à Becket, was said to have been taken prisoner on a pilgrimage to the Holy Land and eventually released from captivity by his captor's daughter, who then made her way to London, found him and married him. In many of the ballad variants she is given the odd name of Susie Pye.

The set given here is collated from Child's texts, together with two Scots versions printed by Gavin Greig, who knew the song well enough to comment, 'The tune is a grand specimen of old-world melody.' The melody given here is accordingly the one published by Greig from the singing, in 1904, of J. D. Knowles of Buckie.

borrow: rescue   **gin:** if

CHILD #53   ROUD #40

DURHAM GAOL

Ye'll all hev heard of Dur-ham Gaol But it wad ye much sur-prise To see the priso-ners
yard is built a - round wi' walls_ Se no-ble and se strang Whe iv - er gans there

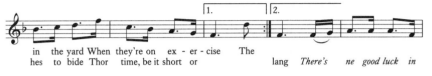

in the yard When they're on ex - er - cise The
hes to bide Thor time, be it short or lang *There's ne good luck in*

Dur-ham Gaol There's ne good luck at all What is bread and skil-ly for But just to make ye small?

Ye'll all hev heard of Durham Gaol
But it wad ye much surprise
To see the prisoners in the yard
When they're on exercise
The yard is built around wi' walls
Se noble and se strang
Whe iver gans there hes to bide
Thor time, be it short or lang

There's ne good luck in Durham Gaol
There's ne good luck at all
What is breed and skilly for
But just te make ye small?

When ye gan to Durham Gaol
They'll find ye wiv employ
They'll dress ye up se dandy

In a suit o' cordyroy
They'll fetch a cap wivoot a peak
An' niver ax your size
An' like your suit, it's cordyroy
An' comes doon ower your eyes

The forst month is the warst iv all
    Your feelins they will try
There's nowt but two greet lumps o' wood
    On which ye hae to lie
Then eftor that ye get a bed
    But it is hard as stanes
At neet ye dorsen't make a turn
    For fear ye break some banes

All kinds o' wark there's gannen on
    Upon them noble flats
Teasin oakum, makin balls
    An' weavn coco mats
When ye gan in ye may be thin
    But they can make ye thinner
If your oakum isn't teased
    They's sure to stop your dinner

The shoes ye get is often tens
    The smallest size is nine
They're big enough to make a skiff
    For Boyd upon the Tyne
An' if ye should be caud at neets
    Just make yoursels at hyem

Lap your claes around your shoes
　　An' get inside o' them

Ye'll get your meat and claes for nowt
　　Your hoose an' firin' free
All your meat's browt te the door
　　Hoo happy ye should be!
There's soap and towel an' wooden speun
　　An' a little bairnie's pot
They fetch ye papers every week
　　For ye to clean your bot.

THOMAS ARMSTRONG (1848–1920) was a Durham miner, poet and songmaker, compelled to entertain in order to feed his fourteen children and satisfy his prodigious thirst. His numerous songs sit on the border between orality and composition.

How did Armstrong come to be gaoled? In 1878, he was taken before the local magistrates by a notoriously mean checkweighman (locally called a keeker) at the Oakey colliery, whom he had offended in his song 'Oakey's Keeker'. This may have been for criminal libel, and newspaper reports indicate that the case was laughed out of court. So it is possible that the six months that Armstrong (according to his son) spent in Durham Gaol, as commemorated in this song, were for debt rather than for crime. But the mention in the song of oakum picking and plank beds, together with the bad food and humiliating clothing, are more suggestive of a punitive sentence than of the debtor's wing which every gaol had.

Many of Armstrong's songs were printed as broadsides for sale, and the orthography of the present text is his own. The tune he gave for it is the Scots song 'Nae Guid Luck Aboot the Hoose'. Both are taken here from A. L. Lloyd's classic study *Come All Ye Bold Miners*.

breed and skilly: bread and gruel
gannen: going

claes: clothes
small: thin

THE GALLOWS

Ballad literature, while generally unflinching about the fatal ends of its heroes and villains, rarely goes into any detail beyond the fact of hanging. But the songs in this section make dramatic use of the arbitrary and haphazard road from the dock to the gallows.

The casual and unjust nature of capital trials was notorious. In 1714, Pope wrote:

> The hungry Judges soon the Sentence sign,
> And Wretches hang that Jury-men may Dine.

The public hangings that followed, although defended as a deterrent, were above all a spectacle. In the 1850s, Thomas Hardy, still a boy, witnessed two of the last public hangings at Dorchester without conscious emotion; but he came to realize that the sight had scarred him for life, particularly on the second occasion, when he watched through his father's telescope as, three miles distant, the condemned man's body dropped.

The law had more than one way of taking life. The ringing prohibition in the 1689 Bill of Rights of 'cruell and unusuall punishments' seems to have gone unheeded. In addition to decapitation and hanging (accompanied, for male traitors, by drawing and quartering, while women convicted of treason, including the petty treasons of coining or murdering their husbands, could until 1790 be burnt alive), the law until 1772 allowed the pressing to death of prisoners who, to avoid forfeiture of their estates, would not plead to the charge against them. Although other cruel punishments, including flogging and maiming, were used until at least the eighteenth century (flogging was in fact reintroduced in 1863 by the Garroters Act, and birching of minors continued on the Isle of Man until 1978, when it was stopped by the European Court of Human Rights), they feature rarely in traditional song. By the 1840s, after decades of argument, the Bloody Code of capital offences with which England had entered the nineteenth century was reduced to, effectively, murder, treason, arson at military installations, piracy – and (until 1861) sodomy.

Thus the gallows remained an integral part of the legal system both before and after the abolition, in 1868, of public executions. The songs gathered here seem to confirm Hardy's sense that it was the spectacle of the drop (the gibbeting of hanged corpses was ended in 1834) that, as its advocates intended, concentrated the onlooker's mind.

There are whole histories of hanging, but quantifying its use over time is difficult. This is because the number of executions, even in the early nineteenth century when capital offences were at their most numerous, fell well short of the number of death sentences passed by the judges. Thus in 1805, of some 350 felons sentenced to death in England and Wales, no more than 68 – about one-fifth – were hanged. By 1825, the number of death sentences passed had climbed to 5,000, but the proportion executed had fallen to less than a twelfth of them. Added to this element of 'glorious uncertainty' (Archdeacon Paley's sadistic phrase for the deterrent value of nearly being hanged) was the bizarre legislative response to the growing abolitionist movement: by the Judgement of Death Act of 1823, English and Welsh judges in capital cases other than murder were empowered, where they considered mercy to be appropriate, to record a sentence of death without actually donning the black cap and pronouncing the sentence. In law, this procedure, which appears to have been used in a very high proportion of male homosexuality cases, had the effect of a reprieve.

For those on whom a death sentence was actually pronounced – in effect, those convicted of murder – living or dying was a lottery. Outside London, petitions to the Home Secretary for clemency poured in on behalf of those of the condemned who could find respectable, or at least literate, local supporters. For London and Middlesex, after each session at the Old Bailey, George IV would be attended at Windsor by senior judges and cabinet ministers to review a list of the condemned and be told what the Recorder of London and the Home Secretary considered should now be done. While the king dozed, occasionally waking to intervene on the side of clemency, the Recorder would write either 'Respited' or 'Law to take its course' against each name.

Lord Ellenborough – no great humanitarian – wrote in his diary in 1828:

I am shocked by the inequality of punishment. At one time a man is hanged because there are few to be hanged and it is some time since an example has been made for his particular offence. At another time a man escapes for the same crime because it is a heavy calendar and there are many to be executed.

THE PRICKLY BUSH

'Hang-man, stay your hand— And stay it for a while— For I think I see— my own dear mo-ther Com-ing o'er yon-der stile Mo-ther have you brought me gold— Or sil-ver to set me free— To save my bo-dy from the cold, cold ground And my neck from the gal-lows tree?'— 'No, I have not brought thee gold— Nor sil-ver to set you free— But I have come to see you hung All on the gal-lows tree' 'O the bush, the prick - ly bush That pricks my heart so sore— If once I get out of that prick - ly bush I'll ne-ver get in it no more.'

'Hangman, stay your hand
And stay it for a while
For I think I see my own dear mother
Coming o'er yonder stile

'Mother have you brought me gold
Or silver to set me free
To save my body from the cold, cold ground
And my neck from the gallows tree?'

255

'No, I have not brought thee gold
Nor silver to set you free
But I have come to see you hung
All on the gallows tree.'

'O the bush, the prickly bush
That pricks my heart so sore
If once I get out of that prickly bush
I'll never get in it no more.'

[*The verses are repeated for father, brother, sister*]

'Hangman, stay your hand
And stay it for a while
For I think I see my true love coming
Over yonder stile

True love, have you brought gold
Or silver to set me free
Or have you come to see me hung
All on the gallows tree?'

'O I have brought you gold
And silver to set you free
I am not come to see thee hung
All on the gallows tree.'

'O the bush, the prickly bush
That pricks my heart so sore

If once I get out of the prickly bush
I'll never get in it no more.'

THIS IS BOTH the simplest and the most tantalizing of ballads, for the young woman who sings it is about to be hanged for something – we are not told what – that she has brought upon herself. Each hope that her family will save her is dashed, until at the very last her true love arrives and buys her freedom. The song has been recovered from English and Scots oral tradition in this almost unvarying shape.

But there are clues which link it to an older backstory. In one variant noted by Child, the true-love, when he arrives, says: 'I have found the golden key . . .'. In another, noted by Baring-Gould, the girl asks each of her family 'Hast brought my golden ball?' These fragments link the song to a body of European legend, sometimes taking the form of a children's play-song, about a girl who has been entrusted on pain of death with a golden ball or key which she has lost: hence the prickly bush, the gallows, the uncaring family and the last-minute rescue.

The versions collected by Gardiner in 1906 in Hampshire, by Sharp in Dorset in 1909, by Alfred Williams in Wiltshire and Oxfordshire in 1916 and many years later in Dorset by Peter Kennedy differ little from the present text. Alfred Williams appended a note to his lyrics:

The song was a favourite of the gipsies who camped in Marston Lane when I was a boy. The principal gipsy, whose name was Archelaus, had three sons, namely, Zephyrus, Adolphus, and Job. They all slept together in a little twig tent, and lived chiefly on hedgehogs. The old man played the fiddle, and sang at the fairs.

The tune given here, taken down by George Gardiner from Charles Chivers of Basingstoke in 1906, was transcribed from his manuscript by Frank Purslow in *The Wanton Seed*.

'Prickly' in southern English speech and song was generally pronounced 'prickle-eye'.

CHILD #95   ROUD #144

MACPHERSON'S FAREWELL

Fare-weel ye dun-geons dark and strang Fare-weel, Fare-weel tae ye Mac-pher-son's time will no' be lang On yon-der gal-lows tree Sae ran-ting-ly, sae wan-ton-ly Sae dain-ti-ly gaed he He played a tune and he danced it round A - blaw the gal-lows tree

Fareweel ye dungeons dark and strang
Fareweel, fareweel tae ye.
Macpherson's time will no' be lang
On yonder gallows tree

    Sae rantingly, sae wantonly
    Sae daintily gaed he
    He played a tune and he danced it round
    Ablaw the gallows tree

There's some come here tae see me hang'd
And some tae buy my fiddle
But afore that I will part wi' her
I'll brak her through the middle

And he's took his fiddle in baith his hands
And brak it ower a stane

Saying, 'There's nae hand shall play on thee
When I am dead and gane.'

The reprieve was coming o'er the Brig o' Banff
Tae set Macpherson free
But they put the clock a quarter afore
And they hang'd him frae the tree

Sae rantingly, sae wantonly
Sae daintily gaed he
He played a tune and he danced it round
Ablaw the gallows tree.

MACPHERSON, a well-known Scottish brigand, was captured at Keith Market in 1700 and hanged at the Cross of Banff. He was also well known as a fiddle-player, and his defiant end became the subject of numerous broadsides, one of which Robert Burns, not altogether successfully, recast. His end, at least in the song, is dramatic not only because of his virtuosity but because of the perfidy of the sheriff in moving the hands of the town clock, so that Macpherson could be turned off, as the expression was, before a reprieve arrived.

The present text, with its tune, is taken from the composite version made by Norman Buchan from the singing of two Scots Travellers, Jimmy McBeath and Davy Stewart, but adopts Burns's opening stanza.

ablaw: below

ROUD #2160

GEORDIE

'Will ye gang to the Hie-lands, my__ bon-ny bon-ny love Will ye gang to the Hie-lands wi'__ Geor - die It's__ ye'll tak' the high road and I'll__ tak' the low And I'll be in the Hie - lands a - fore ye.'

'Will ye gang to the Hielands, my bonny bonny love
Will ye gang to the Hielands wi' Geordie
It's ye'll tak' the high road and I'll tak' the low
And I'll be in the Hielands afore ye.'

'I would far sooner stay by the bonny banks o' Spey
And see a' the fish boats rowing
Before I would go to yon high Hieland hills
And hear a' your white kye lowing.'

He hadna been in the high Hieland hills
A month but barely two o
Before he was cast in a prison sae strang
For hunting the deer and the roe o

'O where will I find a bonny wee boy
That will run an errand swiftly
That will run unto the bonny Bog o' Gight
Wi' a letter to Gightie's lady?'

'Here am I, a bonny wee boy
That will run an errand swiftly
And I will run tae the bonny Bog o' Gight
Wi' a letter to Gightie's lady.'

When that he cam where the grass grew lang
He slacked his shoes and ran o
And whan he cam where the bridge was broke
He bent his bow and swam o

And when that he cam to Gightie's gates
He neither did chap nor call o
He's bent his bow right close to his chest
And jumped right o'er the wall o

When that she looked the letter upon
A loud loud laugh laughed she o
But ere she had the half o't read
The salt tear blinded he e'e o

'Go saddle me the black,' she said
'The brown rides ne'er so boldly
And I will ride tae Edinburgh toon
Tae borrow the life o' my Geordie.'

When that she cam tae yon ford-mouth
The boatman wasna ready
But she clasped her high horse round the neck
And she swam the river shortly

Whan that she cam to Edinburgh toon
The nobles they stood mony
And every one his hat upon his heid
But hat in hand stood her Geordie

'O has he killed or has he brunt
Or has he robbèd any
Or what has my love Geordie done
That he's to be hangit shortly?'

'He hasna killed nor has he brunt
Nor has he robbèd any
But he's been a-hunting the king's own deer
And he's to be hangit shortly.'

'Will the yellow gold buy off my bonny love
Will the yellow gold buy off my Geordie?
It's five hundred crowns if ye wad pay down
Then you'll get the hat on your Geordie.'

She's ta'en the mantle frae her neck
Spread it out fu' bonny
Ta'en the hat frae Geordie's hand
Tae beg for the life o' her Geordie

Some ga'e her crowns and some ga'e her pounds
And some ga'e her hundreds mony
And the king himsel's gi'en a hundred more
To pay the hat on her Geordie

And when she was on her high horse sat
And in behind her Geordie
The bird ne'er sang sae sweetly on the bush
As she did behind her Geordie

'First I was lady o' bonny Auchendoon
Next I was lady o' Gartly
But noo I'm guidwife o' the bonny Bog o' Gight
And I've begged for the life o' my Geordie.'

THE BALLAD OF GEORDIE has been collected in a bewildering range of versions, but with essentially one of two narrative strands. Almost all of them open with Geordie already condemned to be executed. In the many versions collected in southern and eastern England (Sharp found eight in Somerset alone), he has confessed to stealing the king's deer; his wife's attempts to secure a reprieve fail and he is left to hang in golden chains. The versions found in Scotland are both more dramatic and more specific. Geordie is commonly identified in them as the laird of the Bog of Gight (placing his home at Castle Gordon, near Fochabers on the Spey), and several of the variants begin by recording a battle in which Sir Charles Hay has been killed and Geordie convicted of killing him. In most, however, he has been caught poaching deer. In contrast to the English tradition, his wife begs in the street and, improbably, collects enough gold to secure his release.

The present version adopts the Scots narrative, using the text recorded by Gavin Greig circa 1910 together with a tune that Greig did not print at the time but identified as a probable source of 'Loch Lomond'. It is taken here from the version learnt by Ewan MacColl from Betsy Henry of Auchterader in Perthshire.

chap: knock, rap   **borrow:** rescue, ransom

CHILD #209   ROUD #90

SAM HALL

Oh my name it is Sam Hall
Sammy Hall
My name it is Sam Hall
Sammy Hall
My name it is Sam Hall
And I hate you one and all
You're a bunch of bastards all
Damn your eyes

They said I killed a man
Killed a man
They said I killed a man
Killed a man
I hit him on the head
With a great big lump of lead
And now the bastard's dead
Damn his eyes

The parson he came in
He came in
The parson he came in
He came in
The parson he came in
With his tale of mortal sin
And I kicked him on the shin
Damn his eyes

So it's up the steps I go
Up I go
It's up the steps I go
Up I go
It's up the steps I go
With my mates all down below
Saying, 'Sam, we told you so.'
Damn their eyes

They hung me from the tree
From the tree
They hung me from the tree
From the tree
They hung me from the tree
I said 'Won't you set me free
The suspense is killing me
Damn your eyes.'

So it's here I am in hell
Am in hell
So it's here I am in hell

Am in hell
So here I am in hell
But it's all a bloody sell
'Cos the parson's here as well
Damn his eyes.

JACK HALL, chimney-sweep and burglar, was hanged at
Tyburn in 1707 with two accomplices. He was a well-known
London villain, and the ballad-mongers used a verse-form and
tune which had become widely known in a ballad celebrating
Admiral Benbow's heroic death in battle against the French
in 1702:

Come all you sailors bold,
Lend an ear, lend an ear

Neither ballad was, however, the source of the format: it
had been used for a broadside (a very poor maudlin effort) on
the execution of Sir Walter Raleigh in 1618, and again in the
Civil War for the rallying song composed for the Diggers by
their spokesman Gerard Winstanley:

You noble Diggers all
Stand up now, stand up now

The original 'Jack Hall' song at least had an elegiac quality
('My life will pay for all when I die'), and several variants of
it have turned up in oral tradition. But in the mid-nineteenth
century, it was turned by the stage comedian G. W. Ross into a

raucous burlesque, making Sam Hall a foul-mouthed sociopath, and it's principally in this form that it has come down to us.

The present version was learnt by Bill Sedley (the father of one of the editors) during war service in the Eighth Army. Other versions end slightly differently:

> In heaven now I dwell
> But it's all a bloody sell
> For the whores are all in hell . . .

The tune is Chappell's tune for 'Admiral Benbow'.

ROUD #369

EPILOGUE

WHO KILLED COCK ROBIN?

'Who killed Cock Robin?'
'I,' said the sparrow,
'With my bow and arrow
I killed Cock Robin.'

All the birds of the air
Fell a-sighing and a-sobbing
When they heard of the death of poor Cock Robin
When they heard of the death of poor Cock Robin

'Who saw him die?'
'I,' said the fly,
'With my little eye
I saw him die.'

'Who caught his blood?'
'I,' said the fish,
'With my little dish
I caught his blood.'

'Who'll make his shroud?'
'I,' said the beetle,
'With my little needle
I'll make his shroud.'

'Who'll dig his grave?'
'I,' said the owl,
'With my spade and trowel
I'll dig his grave.'

'Who'll be the parson?'
'I,' said the rook,
'With my little book
I'll be the parson.'

'Who'll be the clerk?'
'I,' said the lark,
'If 'tis not in the dark
I'll be the clerk.'

'Who'll carry him to the grave?'
'I,' said the kite,
'If 'tis not in the night
I'll carry him to the grave.'

'Who'll carry the link?'
'I,' said the linnet,
'I'll fetch it in a minute
I'll carry the link.'

'Who'll be chief mourner?'
'I,' said the dove,
'As I mourn for my love
I'll be chief mourner.'

'Who'll bear the pall?'
'We,' said the wren,
'Both the cock and the hen
We'll bear the pall.'

'Who'll sing a psalm?'
'I,' said the thrush,
'As he sat in a bush
I'll sing a psalm.'

'Who'll toll the bell?'
'I,' said the bull,
'Because I can pull
So Cock Robin farewell.'

All the birds of the air
Fell a-sighing and a-sobbing
When they heard of the death of poor Cock Robin
When they heard of the death of poor Cock Robin.

ALTHOUGH THIS ELEGY on the death of a songbird has trav-
elled down the generations as a nursery song (the London
printer Dicey issued it as *Cock Robin, a pretty gilded Toy for*
either Girl or Boy), it is as much about the unity of life as it
is about an isolated death, for the whole animal kingdom is
touched by grief.

The song is older than we can tell: a fifteenth-century
stained-glass window at Buckland Rectory in Gloucestershire
shows a robin killed by an arrow. Why he was killed we never
learn, though in one variant of the song the sparrow is hanged
for his crime. But the likelihood is that the song owes its origin
simply to the fact that the natural colour of the robin's breast
resembles a bloodstain.

There is evidence that 'Who Killed Cock Robin?', like
'The Derby Ram', was sung by soldiers in the trenches during
the Great War to relieve the unbearable tension of waiting for
an incoming bombardment or the order to advance. The poet
Edmund Blunden, like many other officers, failed to understand
why his men preferred to sing songs characterized not by inspira-
tional sentiments but by prolonged repetition. Underscoring this
usage, the 1924 *Daily Express* songbook contained what it called
the 'army version' of the song, padded out with a second chorus.

The version used here is based on the illustrated octavo
chapbook, *An Elegy on the Death and Burial of Cock Robin*,

published by the master-printer James Kendrew of York, circa 1820, a verse to a page.

link: a torch made of pitch and tow

ROUD #494

SELECT BIBLIOGRAPHY

Ashton, John, *Modern Street Ballads* (London, 1888)

Bell, Robert, *Ballads and Songs* (London, 1856)

Bronson, Bertrand Harris, *The Traditional Tunes of the Child Ballads*, 4 vols (Princeton, NJ, 1959–72)

—, *The Singing Tradition of Child's Popular Ballads* (Princeton, NJ, 1976)

Bruce, J. Collingwood, and John Stokoe, *Northumbrian Minstrelsy* (Newcastle, 1882)

Buchan, Norman, *101 Scottish Songs* (Glasgow, 1962)

Buchan, Peter, *Ballads of the North of Scotland* (Edinburgh, 1828)

Chappell, William, *Old English Popular Music*, 2 vols (London, 1838–40)

Child, Francis James, *The English and Scottish Popular Ballads*, 5 vols (Boston, MA, 1882–98)

Christie, William, *Traditional Ballad Airs* (Edinburgh, 1876)

Dixon, James, *Ancient Poems, Ballads and Songs* (London, 1846)

Doerflinger, William Main, *Shantymen and Shantyboys* (New York, 1951)

Gardiner, George, *Folk Songs from Hampshire* (London, 1909)

Greig, Gavin, *Folk-song of the North-east* (Buchan, 1907–11)

Henry, Sam, *Songs of the People*, in the *Northern Constitution* newspaper (Limavady, 1923–38)

Hugill, Stan, *Shanties from the Seven Seas* (London and New York, 1961)

Jamieson, Robert, *Popular Ballads and Songs*, 2 vols (Edinburgh, 1806)

Johnson, James, *The Scots Musical Museum*, 2 vols (Edinburgh, 1787–1803)

Kidson, Frank, *Traditional Tunes* (Oxford, 1891)

Kinloch, George, *Ancient Scottish Ballads* (Edinburgh, 1827)

Lloyd, A. L., *Come All Ye Bold Miners* [1952] (London, 1978)

Maidment, James, *North Countrie Garland* (Edinburgh, 1824)

Motherwell, William, *Minstrelsy: Ancient and Modern* (Boston, MA, 1827)

O'Lochlainn, Colm, *Irish Street Ballads* (Dublin, 1939)

—, *More Irish Street Ballads* (Dublin, 1965)

Percy, Thomas, *Reliques of Ancient English Poetry*, 3 vols (London, 1765)

Purslow, Frank, *Marrowbones* (London, 1965)

—, *The Wanton Seed* (London, 1968)

Roud, Steve, and Julia Bishop, *The New Penguin Book of English Folk Songs* (London, 2012)

Scott, Walter, *The Minstrelsy of the Scottish Border*, 3 vols (London and Edinburgh, 1802–3)

Seeger, Peggy, and Ewan MacColl, *The Singing Island* (London, 1960)

Sharp, Cecil, *Collection of English Folk Songs*, ed. Maud Karpeles, 2 vols (London, 1974)

Sharpe, Charles, *A Ballad Book* (Edinburgh and London, 1823)

Smith, Robert, *The Scottish Minstrel*, 6 vols (Edinburgh, 1820–24)

Thomson, William, *Orpheus Caledonius* (London, 1725; 2nd edn, 2 vols, 1733)

Williams, Alfred, *Folk Songs of the Upper Thames* (London, 1923)

BROADSIDE PRINTERS

Catnach, James, Monmouth Court, Seven Dials, London, *c.* 1813–38

Dicey, Cluer, Aldermary and Bow Churchyards, London, 1720 onwards

Harkness, James, Church Street, Preston, *c.* 1840–66

Kendrew, James, then John (York, *c.* 1803–48), *York Publications* [BL #1870.c.2]